A **SÉRIE BRASIL – Ensino Médio** oferece conteúdo completo em todos os sentidos e integra objetos digitais aos materiais impressos. Acesse o portal exclusivo da coleção e aproveite o que a Editora do Brasil preparou para você.

Portal exclusivo da coleção:
**www.seriebrasilensinomedio.com.br**

### Instruções para acesso aos conteúdos digitais

Acesse o portal exclusivo da coleção (www.seriebrasilensinomedio.com.br) e digite seu *e-mail* e senha. Caso ainda não os tenha, faça o cadastro. Digite o código abaixo para liberar o acesso:

2368559A2090740

Esse código libera o acesso dos conteúdos digitais relativos à matéria e ao ano deste livro. Informamos que esse código é pessoal e intransferível. Guarde-o com cuidado, pois é a única forma de acesso ao conteúdo restrito do portal.

# ENSINO MÉDIO
# INGLÊS
## Your Turn

**2**

### Gisele Aga
Licenciada em Letras pelas Faculdades Metropolitanas Unidas (FMU). Autora de livros didáticos de Língua Inglesa para os anos finais do Ensino Fundamental, autora de materiais didáticos para programas bilíngues, editora de conteúdos didáticos, professora de Língua Inglesa para o Ensino Médio na rede particular de ensino e professora de Língua Inglesa em cursos de idiomas.

### Adriana Saporito
Licenciada em Letras, com habilitação em Tradutor e Intérprete – Português e Inglês – pela Faculdade Ibero-Americana de Letras e Ciências Humanas. Professora de Literatura Brasileira, Língua Portuguesa e Língua Inglesa da rede particular de ensino, autora de livros de Língua Inglesa para Ensino Fundamental e Educação para Jovens e Adultos (EJA), editora de conteúdos didáticos.

### Carla Maurício
Bacharel e licenciada em Letras pela Universidade Federal do Rio de Janeiro (UFRJ). Professora de Língua Inglesa da rede particular de ensino, editora de conteúdos didáticos, autora de livros de Língua Inglesa para os anos finais do Ensino Fundamental e do Ensino Médio.

2ª edição
São Paulo – 2016

COMPONENTE CURRICULAR
LÍNGUA ESTRANGEIRA
MODERNA – INGLÊS
2º ANO
ENSINO MÉDIO

© Editora do Brasil S.A., 2016
*Todos os direitos reservados*

**Direção geral:** Vicente Tortamano Avanso
**Direção adjunta:** Maria Lúcia Kerr Cavalcante Queiroz

**Direção editorial:** Cibele Mendes Curto Santos
**Gerência editorial:** Felipe Ramos Poletti
**Supervisão editorial:** Erika Caldin
**Supervisão de arte, editoração e produção digital:** Adelaide Carolina Cerutti
**Supervisão de direitos autorais:** Marilisa Bertolone Mendes
**Supervisão de controle de processos editoriais:** Marta Dias Portero
**Supervisão de revisão:** Dora Helena Feres
**Consultoria de iconografia:** Tempo Composto Col. de Dados Ltda.
**Licenciamentos de textos:** Cinthya Utiyama, Jennifer Xavier, Paula Harue Tozaki, Renata Garbellini
**Coordenação de produção CPE:** Leila P. Jungstedt

**Concepção, desenvolvimento e produção:** Triolet Editorial e Mídias Digitais
**Diretora executiva:** Angélica Pizzutto Pozzani
**Diretor de operações:** João Gameiro
**Gerente editorial:** Denise Pizzutto
**Editor de texto:** Camilo Adorno
**Assistente editorial:** Tatiana Pedroso
**Preparação e revisão:** Amanda Andrade, Carol Gama, Érika Finati, Flávia Venezio, Flávio Frasqueti, Gabriela Damico, Juliana Simões, Leandra Trindade, Mayra Terin, Patrícia Rocco, Regina Elisabete Barbosa, Sirlei Pinochia
**Projeto gráfico:** Triolet Editorial/Arte
**Editoras de arte:** Ana Onofri, Paula Belluomini
**Assistentes de arte:** Beatriz Landiosi (estag.), Lucas Boniceli (estag.)
**Ilustradora:** Suryara Bernardi
**Cartografia:** Allmaps
**Iconografia:** Pamela Rosa (coord.), Clarice França, Joanna Heliszkowski
**Fonografia:** Maximal Estúdio
**Tratamento de imagens:** Fusion DG
**Capa:** Beatriz Marassi
**Imagem de capa:** Inti St Clair/Getty Images

---

**Dados Internacionais de Catalogação na Publicação (CIP)**
**(Câmara Brasileira do Livro, SP, Brasil)**

Your Turn, 2 : ensino médio / Gisele Aga, Adriana Saporito, Carla Maurício. – 2. ed. – São Paulo : Editora do Brasil, 2016. – (Série Brasil : ensino médio)

Componente curricular: Língua estrangeira moderna – Inglês
ISBN 978-85-10-06465-1 (aluno)
ISBN 978-85-10-06466-8 (professor)

1. Inglês (Ensino médio) I. Saporito, Adriana.
II. Maurício, Carla. III. Título. IV. Série.

16-05818        CDD-420.7

**Índice para catálogo sistemático:**
1. Inglês : Ensino médio    420.7

Reprodução proibida. Art. 184 do Código Penal e Lei n. 9.610 de 19 de fevereiro de 1998.
Todos os direitos reservados

2016
Impresso no Brasil

2ª edição / 1ª impressão, 2016

**Impressão e acabamento:** Intergraf Ind. Gráfica Eireli.

Rua Conselheiro Nébias, 887 – São Paulo/SP – CEP 01203-001
Fone: (11) 3226-0211 – Fax: (11) 3222-5583
www.editoradobrasil.com.br

Todos os esforços foram feitos no sentido de localizar e contatar os detentores dos direitos das músicas reproduzidas no CD que integra a coleção *Your Turn*. Mediante manifestação dos interessados, a Editora do Brasil terá prazer em providenciar eventuais regularizações.

**Imagem de capa:**
Jogo de basquete.

# APRESENTAÇÃO

Caro aluno,

É com enorme satisfação que apresentamos esta coleção. Nós a concebemos tendo em mente você como aluno e como cidadão local e global. Levamos em conta suas necessidades e expectativas em relação ao aprendizado da língua inglesa e todos os benefícios que esse conhecimento poderá trazer para sua vida social e profissional.

Sabemos que o novo milênio necessita cada vez mais de pessoas autônomas e solidárias, que tenham consciência do espaço que ocupam, do meio em que vivem e da sociedade que desejam construir. Portanto, faz-se necessário uma nova postura perante si mesmo, o outro e a realidade. A língua inglesa ocupa papel essencial nesse cenário, uma vez que é o idioma oficial dos negócios, das comunicações, das tecnologias, enfim, do mundo globalizado.

Diante disso, esta coleção oferece a você a oportunidade de entrar em contato com o inglês vivo e real por meio de textos orais e escritos sobre diversos assuntos e provenientes de várias partes do mundo. Você será convidado a refletir sobre suas experiências, suas expectativas e seus posicionamentos como cidadão da comunidade e do planeta em que vive.

Você terá também a oportunidade de produzir textos e participar de projetos que estimulam a parceria, o trabalho colaborativo e o compartilhamento de experiências e conhecimentos. Enfim, você será convidado a assumir o papel de protagonista de seu aprendizado.

Nós, autoras, acreditamos firmemente que oferecemos a você uma coleção rica em diversidade, informação, conhecimento e, especialmente, em prática da língua inglesa viva e atual. Temos plena convicção de que você se apropriará de um aprendizado que lhe trará oportunidades positivas e enriquecedoras em um futuro breve.

Agora é com você! Esperamos que aproveite ao máximo a coleção.

**As autoras**

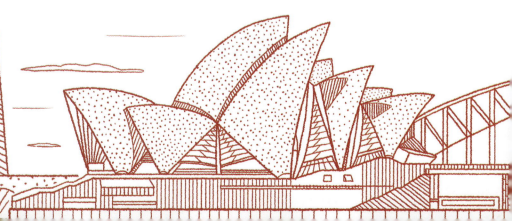

# Conheça o livro

As unidades do seu livro estão organizadas por seções. Conheça um pouco mais sobre elas a seguir.

**Interdisciplinaridade**
Este ícone aponta as disciplinas com as quais a unidade dialoga.

**Starting Out**
Esta seção tem como principais objetivos introduzir o tema que será apresentado e aprofundado ao longo da unidade, bem como ativar seu conhecimento prévio sobre o gênero textual ao qual você será exposto.

**Opening Pages**
Seção que inicia a unidade e tem por objetivo ativar seu conhecimento prévio acerca do tema que será trabalhado, através da exploração de uma imagem. Nessas páginas você também conhecerá os objetivos da unidade.

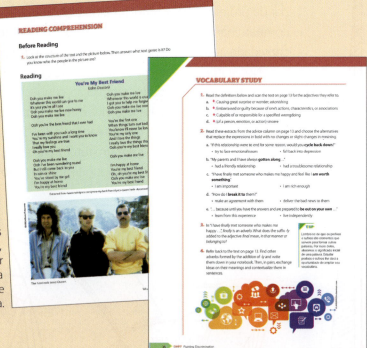

**Reading Comprehension**
Nesta seção, você será exposto a textos escritos de diferentes gêneros e origens, podendo desenvolver sua habilidade de leitura para compreensão geral e detalhada.

**Vocabulary Study**
Aqui você terá a oportunidade de estudar a língua a partir de contextos em uso presentes nos textos da seção anterior, desenvolvendo, assim, o vocabulário de maneira contextualizada.

## Language in Context

Nesta seção, você poderá observar a língua e deduzir as regras gramaticais a partir do texto estudado em *Reading Comprehension*. A seção termina com a subseção *Wrapping up*, na qual você é incentivado a usar as regras gramaticais em diferentes atividades orais e escritas.

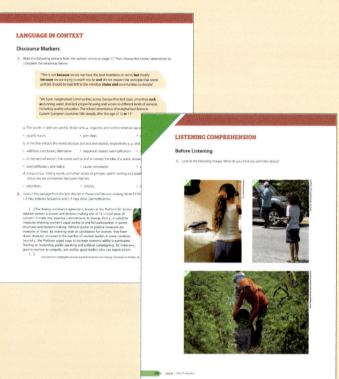

## Listening Comprehension

Aqui você será exposto a textos orais de diferentes gêneros e origens, podendo desenvolver sua habilidade de compreensão global e seletiva, através de variadas estratégias de audição.

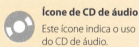

**Ícone de CD de áudio**
Este ícone indica o uso do CD de áudio.

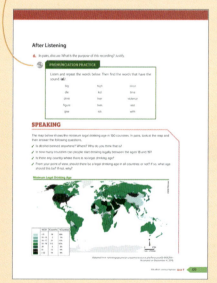

## Speaking

Nesta seção, você participará de atividades que promovem a produção oral através da discussão de assuntos sobre o tema da unidade, usando o vocabulário e as estruturas gramaticais estudadas previamente.

## Writing

Aqui você produzirá textos escritos do mesmo gênero analisado em *Reading Comprehension* e colocará em prática o vocabulário e as estruturas gramaticais estudadas na unidade, levando em consideração o propósito da produção, o público-alvo e as características do gênero.

## Self-Assessment

Ao final de cada unidade, você poderá refletir e avaliar seu processo de desenvolvimento, conscientizando-se em relação aos conhecimentos adquiridos e ao que pode ser ainda aperfeiçoado.

# Conheça o livro

A coleção conta ainda com os seguintes apêndices:

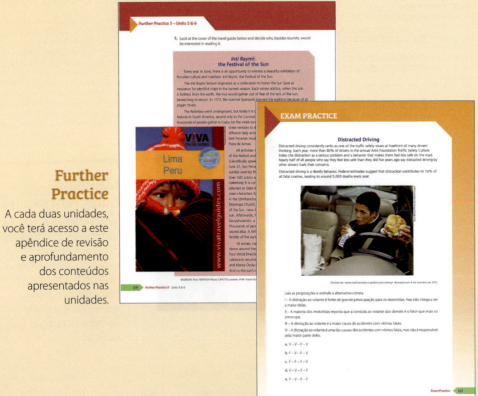

### Further Practice
A cada duas unidades, você terá acesso a este apêndice de revisão e aprofundamento dos conteúdos apresentados nas unidades.

### Exam Practice
Apêndice com questões semelhantes às das provas do Enem, também apresentado a cada duas unidades.

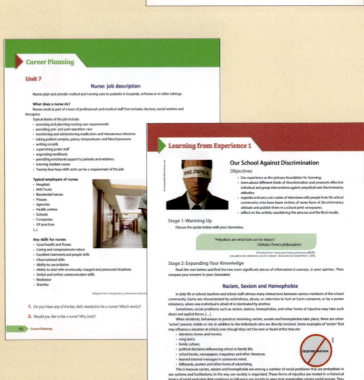

### Career Planning
Aqui você poderá ler e refletir sobre algumas profissões relacionadas aos temas das unidades.

### Learning from Experience
Neste apêndice, você terá a oportunidade de vivenciar experiências concretas de aprendizagem por meio de projetos interdisciplinares relacionados aos temas das unidades.

## Studying for Enem
Através destas páginas, você poderá resolver as questões oficiais do Enem.

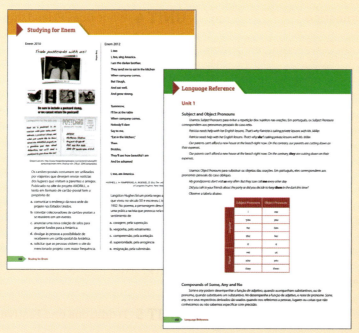

## Language Reference
Apêndice de aprofundamento dos conteúdos linguísticos apresentados nas unidades, com quadros, exemplos e atividades.

Você terá acesso ainda às transcrições dos áudios, à lista de verbos irregulares e ao glossário.

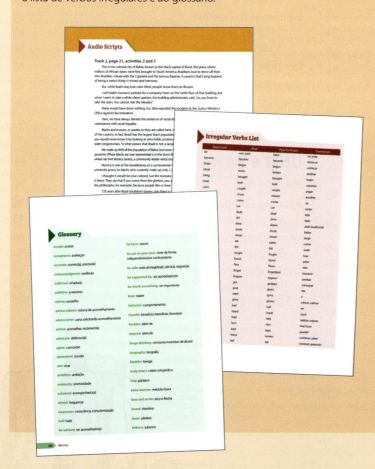

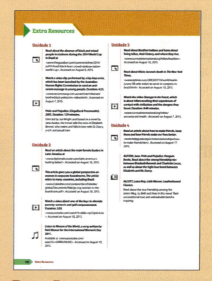

## Extra Resources
Para que você possa consolidar seu aprendizado ou ainda ter acesso a novos conhecimentos além daqueles estudados em aula, recomendamos alguns artigos, vídeos, filmes etc.

**Atenção!**
Não escreva no livro. Todos os exercícios devem ser resolvidos no caderno.

# Sumário

**UNIT 1** Fighting Discrimination ..................... 10
Starting Out ........................................................... 12
Reading Comprehension ...................................... 13
    Dear Abby ........................................................ 13
Vocabulary Study ................................................. 16
    Suffix -ly ........................................................... 16
Language in Context ............................................ 17
    Subject and Object Pronouns ......................... 17
    Compounds with Some, Any and No .............. 18
Listening Comprehension .................................... 20
Speaking ................................................................ 21
Writing ................................................................... 22
Self-Assessment ................................................... 23

**UNIT 2** Women in Power ..................................... 24
Starting Out ........................................................... 26
Reading Comprehension ...................................... 27
    Empowering girls through education
    is best achieved by the member states ......... 27
Vocabulary Study ................................................. 30
    Suffixes -ment, -ance ....................................... 30
Language in Context ............................................ 31
    Discourse Markers .......................................... 31
Listening Comprehension .................................... 34
Speaking ................................................................ 35
Writing ................................................................... 36
Self-Assessment ................................................... 37
Further Practice 1 – Units 1 & 2 .......................... 38
Exam Practice ....................................................... 43

**UNIT 3** They Claim for Respect ......................... 44
Starting Out ........................................................... 46
Reading Comprehension ...................................... 47
    Mário Juruna .................................................... 47
Vocabulary Study ................................................. 50
    Word Groups .................................................... 50
Language in Context ............................................ 51
    Relative Pronouns ........................................... 51
    Prepositions of Time ....................................... 53
Listening Comprehension .................................... 54
Speaking ................................................................ 55
Writing ................................................................... 56
Self-Assessment ................................................... 57

**UNIT 4** What Does Friendship Mean to You? ... 58
Starting Out ........................................................... 60
Reading Comprehension ...................................... 61
    You're My Best Friend (John Deacon) ............ 61
Vocabulary Study ................................................. 64
    Phrasal Verbs ................................................... 64
Language in Context ............................................ 65
    Present Perfect I ............................................... 65
    Present Perfect and Simple Past .................... 66
Listening Comprehension .................................... 68
Speaking ................................................................ 69
Writing ................................................................... 70
Self-Assessment ................................................... 71
Further Practice 2 – Units 3 & 4 .......................... 72
Exam Practice ....................................................... 77

**UNIT 5** Traditions and Festivals ....................... 78
Starting Out ........................................................... 80
Reading Comprehension ...................................... 81
    Cultural Traditions & Festivals in Brazil ......... 81
Vocabulary Study ................................................. 84
    Compound Adjectives ..................................... 84
Language in Context ............................................ 85
    Genitive Case ................................................... 85
    Possessive Adjectives ..................................... 87
Listening Comprehension .................................... 88
Speaking ................................................................ 89
Writing ................................................................... 90
Self-Assessment ................................................... 91

**UNIT 6** My Two Moms ......................................... 92
Starting Out ........................................................... 94
Reading Comprehension ...................................... 95
    Lesbian mothers: My two mums ..................... 95
Vocabulary Study ................................................. 98
    Suffix -phobic ................................................... 98
Language in Context ............................................ 99
    Present Perfect II ............................................. 99
    Comparatives ................................................... 100

Listening Comprehension..................................... 102
Speaking................................................................ 103
Writing.................................................................. 104
Self-Assessment.................................................... 105
Further Practice 3 – Units 5 & 6............................ 106
Exam Practice....................................................... 111

## UNIT 7  Alcohol Consumption .................... 112

Starting Out.......................................................... 114
Reading Comprehension...................................... 115
    Alcohol Use 2012/2013: New Zealand Health Survey..... 115
Vocabulary Study................................................. 118
    Word Families.................................................. 118
Language in Context............................................ 119
    Passive Voice I................................................. 119
Listening Comprehension..................................... 122
Speaking............................................................... 123
Writing.................................................................. 124
Self-Assessment.................................................... 125

## UNIT 8  Child Protection ............................ 126

Starting Out.......................................................... 128
Reading Comprehension...................................... 129
    What is this report about?............................... 129
Vocabulary Study................................................. 132
    Compound Adjectives..................................... 132
Language in Context............................................ 133
    Passive Voice II................................................ 133
Listening Comprehension..................................... 136
Speaking............................................................... 137
Writing.................................................................. 138

Self-Assessment.................................................... 139
Further Practice 4 – Units 7 & 8............................ 140
Exam Practice....................................................... 145

Career Planning.................................................... 146
Learning from Experience.................................... 154
Studying for Enem................................................ 162
Language Reference............................................. 166
Audio Scripts........................................................ 182
Extra Resources.................................................... 187
Irregular Verb List................................................ 189
Glossary................................................................ 190
Bibliography......................................................... 192

Suryara Bernardi

# UNIT 1

# FIGHTING DISCRIMINATION

View Apart/Shutterstock.com

**Nesta unidade você terá oportunidade de:**

- compreender os conceitos de discriminação e preconceito;
- reconhecer os objetivos e algumas características das cartas de aconselhamento e escrever uma;
- compreender uma reportagem sobre discriminação racial na Bahia;
- refletir e discutir sobre o que pode ser feito para combater a discriminação em sua comunidade.

- O que podemos ver na imagem?
- Que relação podemos estabelecer entre a imagem e o título da unidade?

# STARTING OUT  Sociology History

**1.** Match the columns and find out what discrimination and prejudice mean. There is one extra alternative.

a. prejudice

b. discrimination

- The unjust or prejudicial treatment of different categories of people or things, especially on the grounds of race, age, or sex.
- A widely held but fixed and oversimplified image or idea of a particular type of person or thing.
- Preconceived opinion that is not based on reason or actual experience; dislike, hostility, or unjust behavior deriving from unfounded opinions.

Extracted from <www.oxforddictionaries.com/us>. Accessed on August 7, 2015.

**2.** Identify the words we usually associate with discrimination or prejudice.

| ageism | injustice | impartiality |
| racism | xenophobia | honor |
| respect | tolerance | care |
| disdain | regard | homophobia |

**3.** In pairs, discuss the question below and look for the answers that are true for both of you. Then report and justify your answers to the class.

Who or what do you turn to for help when you have doubts or problems?

- I talk to my family and friends.
- I talk to my teachers and counselors.
- I talk to a psychologist or another professional.
- I write about my problems on my blog or in my journal.
- I write to advice columns for advice.
- Others.

12  Unit 1  Fighting Discrimination

# READING COMPREHENSION

## Before Reading

**1.** The letter below was written to an online advice column. Scan the letter and notice that the woman who wrote it didn't sign her real name. Discuss with a classmate and answer: Why do you think she did that?

> **TIP**
>
> Você se lembra da estratégia de leitura chamada *scanning*? O *scanning* consiste em uma leitura rápida do texto em busca de informações específicas, palavras-chaves, frases ou ideias. Quando você utiliza estratégias de leitura como o *scanning*, evita ler palavra por palavra. O *scanning* é muito útil quando queremos, por exemplo, encontrar um número, um determinado nome, uma sigla, uma data, um endereço ou uma fonte.
>
> Baseado em: <www.mundovestibular.com.br/articles/2588/1/TECNICAS-DE-LEITURA-DE-TEXTOS-EM-INGLES---SKIMMIMG-E-SCANNING/Paacutegina1.html>. Acessado em: 22 de outubro de 2015.

## Reading

### Dear Abby

**Teen Fears Telling Racist Parents About Her New Beau**

Jun 27, 2015

**Dear Abby**: I am 18 and live with my parents. I have a part-time job and I also attend a local university. My parents and I have always gotten along, and I have been obedient and respectful of their rules.

I have suffered from depression for years, but now I have finally met someone who makes me happy and feel like I am worth something. Abby, he is of a different race. This doesn't mean anything to me. I know he's a great guy and I really like him. The problem is, my parents are very racist.

They have done so much for me that I feel guilty dating someone they don't approve of. They have told me to never date someone like that. I am torn and ashamed of them, and I don't know what to do.

How do I break it to them? Am I wrong for being with a genuine, amazing guy who finally makes me happy?

— Finally Met Someone in Pennsylvania

---

**Dear Finally Met Someone:** I'm glad you are finally feeling better about yourself as a person, but before discussing this with your parents, it would be better if you separated the issues of your chronic depression and your feelings for this young man.

If this relationship were to end for some reason, would you cycle back down? If your parents react badly – as they may – would you be able to live independently? Are your parents capable of moderating their attitude about people of a different race? And because racism can be universal, how does his family feel about you?

Please consider these questions carefully, because until you have the answers and are prepared to be out on your own, I don't think you should make any announcements.

Adapted from <www.uexpress.com/dearabby/2015/6/27/0/teen-fears-telling-racist-parents-about>. Accessed on August 4, 2015.

> Jeanne Phillips, mais conhecida como Abigail Van Buren ou Abby, iniciou sua carreira como colunista aos 14 anos de idade. *Dear Abby*, a coluna fundada por sua mãe, Pauline Phillips, hoje conta com mais de 110 milhões de leitores em todo o mundo. Jeanne é colunista reconhecida e premiada por vários órgãos e instituições americanas.
>
> Baseado em: <www.uexpress.com.dearabby/about>. Acessado em: 7 de agosto de 2015.

**2.** There are four paragraphs in the teen's letter. Identify the paragraphs where you can find the information below.

   **a.** The girl's feelings about her parents.

   **b.** The problem that the girl is facing.

   **c.** The girl's request for help.

   **d.** The relationship between the girl and her parents.

**3.** Match the statements below to the passages which prove they are true. There is one extra passage.

   **a.** The girl has never disappointed her parents.

   **b.** Since the girl met this guy, she feels happier than ever before.

   **c.** Racism makes absolutely no sense to the girl.

   1. "I know he's a great guy and I really like him."

   2. "I have finally met someone who makes me happy and feel like I am worth something."

   3. "Abby, he is of a different race. This doesn't mean anything to me."

   4. "My parents and I have always gotten along, and I have been obedient and respectful of their rules."

**4.** Based on the following passages from the girl's letter, how would you describe her? Discuss with a classmate.

"I don't know what to do. How do I break it to them? Am I wrong for being with a genuine, amazing guy who finally makes me happy?"

"They have told me to never date someone like that."

"They have done so much for me that I feel guilty dating someone they don't approve of."

Unit 1    Fighting Discrimination

**5.** Read the definition of racism and answer the question below.

**racism**
Prejudice, discrimination, or antagonism directed against someone of a different race based on the belief that one's own race is superior.

Extracted from <www.oxforddictionaries.com/us/definition/american_english/racism>. Accessed on October 22, 2015.

> **TIP**
> Para inferir algo, é necessário ir além da superfície do texto e refletir sobre o que ele nos diz. Muitas vezes, precisamos associar fatos e informações às nossas experiências de vida para chegarmos a alguma conclusão. A inferência combina conhecimentos prévios e pistas que encontramos nos textos. Ela nos permite extrair novas informações a partir daquilo que está escrito. Assim, as conclusões às quais chegamos ao ler um texto serão fundamentadas e coerentes.

If you were Finally Met Someone, how would you cope with that problem?

**6.** Read Abby's answer again and check what you can infer.

a. The girl was advised to reflect carefully on a few issues and to avoid rushing things.

b. Abby states that the causes of the girls' chronicle depression are closely linked to her parents.

c. The girl must feel confident enough to face the consequences of her choice.

d. Abby thinks that the girl will have a hard time if she persists in this relationship.

**7.** Discuss the question below with a classmate. Then share your opinions.

Why do you think people share their problems with a stranger by writing to an advice column?

**8.** Read the sentences below and check the ones that express some of the characteristics of advice letters.

a. Advice letters present problems or ask questions about a specific situation.

b. The language used is formal and the vocabulary is complex.

c. Reply letters express the writer's point of view and his/her personal experiences.

d. Advice letters are usually written in the third person plural.

e. People who write advice letters provide enough details so that reply letters can be helpful.

f. Reply letters contain pieces of advice.

## After Reading

- Racism can wear a friendly face. Can you give some examples to illustrate this? What's your opinion about it?

- In Brazil, racism has been punished by law since 1989. What do you know about it? What is the punishment for racism? Do you think this punishment is strict enough?

- What do you think we can do to avoid discriminatory behavior such as homophobia, ageism, xenophobia etc.?

# VOCABULARY STUDY

1. Read the definitions below and scan the text on page 13 for the adjectives they refer to.
   a. ♦ : Causing great surprise or wonder; astonishing
   b. ♦ : Embarrassed or guilty because of one's actions, characteristics, or associations
   c. ♦ : Culpable of or responsible for a specified wrongdoing
   d. ♦ : (Of a person, emotion, or action) sincere

   Extracted from <www.oxforddictionaries.com/us>. Accessed on August 7, 2015.

2. Read these extracts from the advice column on page 13 and choose the alternatives that replace the expressions in bold with no changes or slight changes in meaning.

   a. "If this relationship were to end for some reason, would you **cycle back down**?"
      • try to face emotional issues
      • fall back into depression

   b. "My parents and I have always **gotten along**…"
      • had a friendly relationship
      • had a troublesome relationship

   c. "I have finally met someone who makes me happy and feel like I **am worth something**."
      • I am important
      • I am rich enough

   d. "How do I **break it to** them?"
      • make an agreement with
      • deliver the bad news to

   e. "… because until you have the answers and are prepared to **be out on your own** …"
      • learn from this experience
      • live independently

3. In "I have *finally* met someone who makes me happy …", *finally* is an adverb. What does the suffix *-ly* added to the adjective *final* mean, *in that manner* or *belonging to*?

4. Refer back to the text on page 13. Find other adverbs formed by the addition of *-ly* and write them down in your notebook. Then, in pairs, exchange ideas on their meanings and contextualize them in sentences.

> **TIP**
>
> Lembre-se de que os prefixos e sufixos são elementos que servem para formar outras palavras. Por meio deles, alteramos o significado inicial de uma palavra. Estudar prefixos e sufixos lhe dará a oportunidade de ampliar seu vocabulário.

Unit 1 — Fighting Discrimination

# LANGUAGE IN CONTEXT

## Subject and Object Pronouns

1. Read the extracts from the advice column on page 13 and pay attention to the words in bold. Then pick out the correct alternatives to complete the sentences that follow.

> "**They** have told **me** to never date someone like that. **I** am torn and ashamed of **them**, and **I** don't know what to do."

> "And because racism can be universal, how does his family feel about **you**?"

> "Abby, **he** is of a different race. This doesn't mean anything to **me**. **I** know **he**'s a great guy and **I** really like **him**."

a. The words in bold are used to replace nouns. They can correspond to the *subjects / modifiers* of clauses or to the *subjects / objects* of verbs.

b. The subject pronouns he, I, and they in the extracts refer respectively to the writer's *father / new beau*, to the writer herself and to *her parents / Abby*.

c. The object pronouns me, him, them, and you refer to elements which *will be mentioned later / have been mentioned before*.

2. Now compose the table below in your notebook and complete it based on the extracts in activity 1.

| Subject Pronouns | Object Pronouns |
|---|---|
| ♦ | ♦ |
| you | you |
| ♦ | ♦ |
| she | her |
| it | it |
| we | us |
| you | ♦ |
| ♦ | ♦ |

3. Read the following poem and pay attention to the pronouns in italics. Then write **S** if they refer to subjects or **O** if they refer to objects.

### Racism Hurts

**By Anonymous, Tucson, AZ**

Stare all *you* ♦ want
I'll gladly return those stares
Whisper behind my back all you want
You seriously think *I* ♦ care?
Try to stereotype *me* ♦ and I'll laugh at *you* ♦
Funny isn't it, how people can be so naive
Funny isn't it, how people think they're being so smart by insulting my race
Who do you think *you* ♦ are?
Make racist comments about me
*It* ♦ hurts but I won't let *you* ♦ know that
*They* ♦ tell me *it* ♦ matters too much
They tell me not to care
Pride in one's country?
Embracing one's heritage?
What connections do I have?
"are you Chinese?"
No
"Are *you* ♦ like Japanese?"
No
"Are you Vietnamese?"
No
"Like what else is there?"
My pride in my country
"Your eyes are so squinty!"
Thank *you* ♦ for noticing
Racism hurts

Extracted from <www.teenink.com/poetry/free_verse/article/486585/Racism-Hurts>. Accessed on August 7, 2015.

## Compounds with Some, Any and No

4. Read the excerpts below and pay attention to the words in bold. Then match the columns to make meaningful sentences about them.

   "I have suffered from depression for years, but now I have finally met **someone** who makes me happy and feel like I am worth **something**. Abby, he is of a different race. This doesn't mean **anything** to me."

   a. The compounds are vague
   b. The compound ending in -*one* refers to people
   c. The compounds derived from *some* are used
   d. The compound derived from *any* is used

   • in affirmative sentences.
   • as they do not refer to any specific person or thing.
   • in a negative sentence.
   • while those ending in -*thing* refer to things.

   For more information on the Compounds, go to Language Reference, page 167.

> *Nobody, no one* e *nothing* são usados em frases afirmativas que expressam sentido negativo.

18 Unit 1 Fighting Discrimination

**5.** Choose the correct alternative to complete the poster.

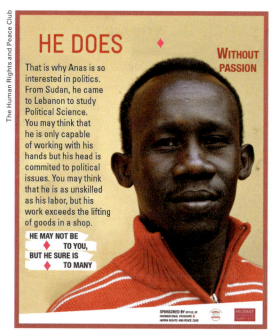

Extracted from <mwtaskforce.wordpress.com/2011/04/26/antiracism-poster-campaign-for-labour-day-2011/>. Accessed on August 7, 2015.

**a.** anything / somebody / anybody

**b.** nothing / somebody / anybody

**c.** nothing / somebody / someone

**6.** Use the words from the box to complete the advice letter below. It was sent to Ellie, an advice columnist in Canada.

> he   him   I   me   someone   they

Ellie
Today's column
September 30, 2014

**Bigotry is wrong, no matter who's preaching it**

Q: So I really like this dude, and I have for almost two years, but ♦ 's mixed race and I'm white.

♦ have a Southern American family who hate it when ♦ see couples that aren't the same race.

They've said they'd disown ♦ if I ever fell for ♦ who wasn't white. But I can't push away these feelings, no matter how hard I try.

I'm happy when I'm with ♦, but I don't feel like giving up my family.
Caught In Middle

Extracted from <ellieadvice.com/bigotry-is-wrong-no-matter-whos-preaching-it/>. Accessed on October 21, 2015.

### WRAPPING UP

Complete the sentences below using some of the information you have discussed in this unit. Then share your opinions with your classmates.

Someone I admire is ♦ because ♦.

Something I'd never tolerate is ♦ because ♦.

# LISTENING COMPREHENSION

## Before Listening

**1.** Look at the images below. What do you think you will listen to?

Colorful Historical Buildings in *Pelourinho*, Salvador, Bahia, Brazil.

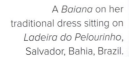

A *Baiana* on her traditional dress sitting on *Ladeira do Pelourinho*, Salvador, Bahia, Brazil.

People playing *Capoeira* in celebration of *Iemanjá*, in Bahia, Brazil.

## Listening

**2.** Listen to a news report from Al Jazeera and check if your prediction was correct.

**3.** Listen to the news report again and answer these questions.

  a. Why is Brazil influenced by African culture?

  b. What happened to Silva when he took a white client to the office of the company he works for?

  c. What did the prosecutor from the Justice Ministry's Office Against Discrimination say to Silva when he reported the incident?

  d. Why did he say that?

  e. According to the state congressman, what makes Brazil a racist place?

**4.** Choose the correct answers and write the full sentences in your notebook.

  a. The purpose of this news report is to *give the reporter's opinion on racial discrimination / present information on racial discrimination in Bahia*.

  b. We can *hear different voices / only hear the reporter's voice*.

## After Listening

What can you infer from this extract? Read and discuss with a classmate.

> "One hundred and twenty years after Brazil abolished slavery, one thing is changing: the awareness that this is, after all, a color-coded country."

## SPEAKING

In small groups:

✓ Discuss: In what ways can we fight discrimination in our community?

✓ Think of at least three actions everybody can take to prevent discrimination at school, in the workplace, or on the streets.

✓ Finally, choose one person from your group to present your ideas to the whole class. Use the expressions from the box.

**USEFUL LANGUAGE**

We think we should…

We'd better…

We know we have to…

We are convinced that…

We really do think that…

# WRITING

Follow the steps below and write an advice letter.

## Planning your advice letter

- Think of a problem or a question you have. It can be related to school issues, family, friends, or relationships.

- If you prefer, make up a problem.

- If possible, visit the website where the advice letter on page 13 was extracted from and read some more letters.

- Take notes of the most common expressions.

## Writing and rewriting your text

- Gather all your ideas and notes and write a draft of your letter in your notebook.

- Don't forget to use the common characteristics of advice letters. If necessary, read the letter on page 13 again. Refer back to activity 8 on page 15, read the characteristics out loud, and identify them in the letter on page 13 once again.

- Choose a classmate to send your letter to.

> **REFLECTING AND EVALUATING**
>
> Go back to your advice letter and make sure you paid enough attention to the following topics:
>
> ✓ Is your problem clear and legible enough?
>
> ✓ Have you offered enough details about your problem?
>
> ✓ Is the language appropriate for the target audience?
>
> ✓ Have you chosen a fictional name?

- Make all the necessary changes and write a clean copy.

- Exchange notebooks and write a reply to the letter you received.

## After writing

- Take back your notebook and read the reply given to your advice letter. Is it helpful?

# SELF-ASSESSMENT

Chegamos ao fim da unidade 1. Convidamos você a refletir sobre seu desempenho até aqui e a responder às questões propostas abaixo, escolhendo uma das seguintes opções:

Sim.   Preciso me preparar mais.

### Questões

- Você é capaz de identificar os diferentes tipos de comportamento discriminatório presentes em nosso cotidiano, discutir os prejuízos que eles causam às pessoas e agir de alguma forma para preveni-los?
- Você se considera apto a ler e compreender uma carta de aconselhamento em língua inglesa, bem como a extrair dela novas informações e reconhecer as características principais inerentes ao gênero?
- Você reúne conhecimentos linguístico-discursivos suficientes para produzir uma carta de aconselhamento em inglês?
- Você se considera preparado para escutar reportagens sobre discriminação e compreender informações específicas?
- Você se julga apto a apresentar oralmente suas ideias, de forma clara e coerente, em relação a medidas preventivas que podem ser tomadas contra situações de discriminação em sua comunidade?

### Refletindo sobre suas respostas

- De que forma suas práticas de aprendizagem no decorrer desta unidade influenciaram suas respostas?
- O que você pode fazer para aprimorar ainda mais os conhecimentos adquiridos nesta unidade?
    a. Procurar conhecer mais sobre os diferentes tipos de discriminação e preconceito, bem como ler o artigo 140 do Código Penal.
    b. Ler mais cartas de aconselhamento e as respostas dadas a elas, para desenvolver melhor minha capacidade de inferência.
    c. Aprofundar meus conhecimentos de língua inglesa, usando recursos diversos, de forma que minha participação nas atividades seja mais ativa.
    d. Outros.

# UNIT 2

# WOMEN IN POWER

**Nesta unidade você terá oportunidade de:**

- refletir sobre a igualdade de direitos entre homens e mulheres e se posicionar criticamente em relação a essa questão;

- reconhecer os objetivos e algumas das características dos artigos de opinião e produzir um;

- compreender trecho de discurso em comemoração ao 100º aniversário do Dia Internacional da Mulher;

- participar ativamente de um debate.

- O que podemos inferir da imagem?
- Podemos relacionar esta foto ao contexto social de hoje? Justifique.

# STARTING OUT

 Sociology / History

**1.** According to the Oxford Dictionary, a *role model* is "a person looked to by others as an example to be imitated."

<small>Extracted from <www.oxforddictionaries.com/us/definition/american_english/role-model?q=role+model>. Accessed on August 8, 2015.</small>

Complete the mind map with words from the box. There are a few extra words.

| dishonor | fame | inspiration | integrity | leadership | negligence | respect | strength | wealth |

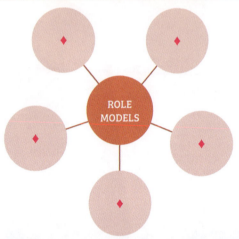

> **TIP**
>
> *Mind maps* (mapas mentais) auxiliam na organização de ideias e são muito usados na confecção de sumários, na análise de assuntos complexos, na apresentação de informações associadas a um tema central etc.
>
> <small>Baseado em: <criatividadeaplicada.com/2007/03/18/mapa-mental-organize-suas-idias/>. Acessado em: 26 de outubro de 2015.</small>

**2.** Who is in the pictures below? Match the columns.

- Malala Yousafzai, Pakistani activist who survived an attempt on her life when she was a young girl and turned out to be a fierce advocate of female rights and education not only in the Middle East but also around the world.

  <small>Based on <edition.cnn.com/2012/10/10/opinion/ghitis-malala-yousufzai>. Accessed on August 12, 2015.</small>

- Aung San Suu Kyi, Myanmarese activist and politician who became internationally famous and recognized after her campaign for democracy in Myanmar.

  <small>Based on <www.forbes.com/profile/aung-san-suu-kyi/>. Accessed on August 12, 2015.</small>

- Zilda Arns, Brazilian pediatrician and aid worker who fought for children, the poor and the elderly in Brazil and abroad. She died in the 2010 earthquake in Haiti.

  <small>Based on <www.pastoraldacrianca.org.br/pt/biografia-dra-zilda>. Accessed on August 12, 2015.</small>

**3.** Why do you think people read opinion articles?

- To find out a person's opinion about a particular issue.
- To have fun.
- To broadcast an event in the neighborhood.
- Others.

# READING COMPREHENSION

## Before Reading

**1.** Scan the opinion article below and find the following information.

   **a.** Name of the author.

   **b.** Name of the periodical in which the article was published.

> **TIP**
>
> Sempre leia os textos mais de uma vez. A cada boa leitura, mais claro ficará o texto. Para tanto, pode ser necessário interromper a leitura em alguns momentos, para refletir sobre o trecho lido. Por isso, volte aos parágrafos anteriores sempre que preciso, até que toda a informação esteja clara para você.

## Reading

### Empowering girls through education is best achieved by the member states

Jana Žitňanská,

18 June 2015

Marking my first anniversary in the European Parliament I have come to realize that all too often we try to focus on issues that are largely distant to Europe's citizens.

This is not because we do not have the best intentions in mind, but mostly because we are trying to reach too far and do not respect the principle that some policies should be best left to the member states and communities to decide.

The topic of girls' empowerment lies at the top of our Women's Rights and Gender Equality Committee's priorities and we will be discussing it in the coming days and weeks.

When I think about girls and empowerment I first and foremost think about the girls who do not have the chance to think about school materials or formal and informal curricula – simply because they have none or cannot even access the education they are entitled to.

We have marginalised communities across Europe that lack basic amenities such as running water, that lack proper housing and access to different kinds of services including quality education. The school attendance of marginalised Roma in Eastern European countries falls steeply after the age of 12 or 13.

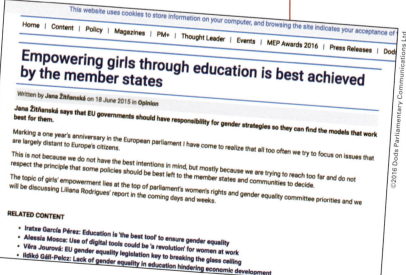

Across Europe, only 15 per cent of Roma have a secondary education. Girls rarely study beyond primary school. A Bulgarian community leader has explained this as due to a lack of role models in a recent article in *The Economist*.

Women in Power **Unit 2**     27

In other news, Slovak and Czech governments have committed themselves to ending discrimination of Roma pupils in their education systems. But they have both failed to do so and are facing proceedings by the European commission over their treatment of Roma school boys and girls.

There is a practice of putting children into segregated classes or simply refusing them the right to quality mainstream education, directing them instead to special schools. We also have thousands of parents whose attempts to get education for their children are rejected because schools do not want or cannot afford appropriate and accessible environments or quality education for children with disabilities.

It is true that very often we face physical barriers when we talk about educating our girls. Certainly, the discussion about girls and their potential and empowerment varies from country to country.

We have member states with segregated schools and we have member states where the discussion on girls in science, technology, engineering and mathematics is vibrant, necessary and genuine.

This is also the reason why I think it is better to leave gender strategies and supervision from gender bodies on member states so that they can discover a model which suits them best. Personally, here in Parliament, I would prefer to have a conversation on the topic I briefly outlined in this article – persistent discrimination and social marginalisation.

There are girls in the EU who are not getting any education at all and these girls should come first and be empowered.

Adapted from <www.theparliamentmagazine.eu/articles/opinion/empowering-girls-through-education-best-achieved-member-states>. Accessed on October 26, 2015.

**marginalised** (UK)
**marginalized** (US)

**marginalisation** (UK)
**marginalization** (US)

**2.** Read the text and write T (True) or F (False).

   a. Some Roma students are rejected by mainstream schools in Eastern European countries.

   b. Slovak and Czech governments have succeeded in ending discrimination against Roma students.

   c. Girls' empowerment policies should be different from country to country depending on the students' necessities.

   d. From 12-13 percent of the marginalized Roma population in Eastern Europe don't go to school.

**3.** Choose the information that is NOT given in the opinion article.

   a. Most Roma girls don't go to high school.

   b. Some communities in Europe lack very basic amenities.

   c. Segregated school classes exist in different countries in Europe, especially in Eastern Europe.

**4.** Jana Žitňanská states that the European Parliament sometimes tries to tell member states what to do and doesn't allow for the peculiarities of that country to determine what is best. Which passage says that?

   a. "[…] mostly because we are trying to reach too far and do not respect the principle that some policies should be best left to the member states and communities to decide."

   b. "[…] I first and foremost think about the girls who do not have the chance to think about school materials or formal and informal curricula - simply because they have none or cannot even access the education they are entitled to."

**5.** Answer the questions below. Then compare your answers to a classmate's.

   a. In the last two paragraphs, the author expresses her point of view. She believes that every EU country should work on policies regarding girls' empowering according to their own realities. Do you think that her suggestion is effective? Justify.

   b. Discrimination and prejudice don't only occur at school, but also in other environments. What forms of discrimination and prejudice do you know about? How do these situations impact the victims? How can we prevent discrimination and prejudice?

**6.** Match the columns to form meaningful sentences about some characteristics of opinion articles.

   a. Opinion articles present the author's

   b. They also present

   c. The main argument is usually in the opening paragraph

   d. The author's own voice is often used

   e. The last paragraph usually reiterates

   1. to convey the message.

   2. perspectives about a current topic.

   3. in order to clearly state the author's point of view.

   4. fact-based points that support the author's arguments.

   5. the author's arguments and viewpoints.

## After Reading

- Are discrimination and segregation common practices in the Brazilian educational system? Explain.

- In your opinion, what are the short-term and long-term benefits of investing in women's education?

- Think about what you already know about the role of women in Brazilian society in the last century. How would you evaluate their progress over the decades in different areas, such as politics, culture, family and career?

# VOCABULARY STUDY

**1.** Refer to the opinion article on page 27 to infer the meaning of these verbs and match the columns. Then use the correct tense of two verbs from the first column to complete the extracts from the books *Little Men* and *Feminism is for Everybody: Passionate Politics*.

- **a.** lack
- **b.** afford
- **c.** reach
- **d.** commit
- **e.** fail

- Be unsuccessful in achieving one's goal
- Pledge or bind (a person or an organization) to a certain course or policy
- Be without or deficient in
- (can/could afford) Have enough money to pay for
- Arrive at; get as far as

Extracted from <www.oxforddictionaries.com/us/>. Accessed on May 25, 2016.

> "Simple, genuine goodness is the best capital to found the business of this life upon. It lasts when fame and money ♦ , and is the only riches we can take out of this world with us." – Louisa May Alcott, *Little Men*

Extracted from <www.goodreads.com/quotes/search?utf8=%E2%9C%93&q=women+fail&commit=Search>. Accessed on October 26, 2015.

> "In a culture which holds the two-parent patriarchal family in higher esteem than any other arrangement, all children feel emotionally insecure when their family does not measure up to the standard. A utopian vision of the patriarchal family remains intact despite all the evidence which proves that the well-being of children is no more secure in the dysfunctional male-headed household than in the dysfunctional female-headed household. Children need to be raised in loving environments. Whenever domination is present love ♦ . Loving parents, be they single or coupled, gay or straight, headed by females or males, are more likely to raise healthy, happy children with sound self-esteem. In future feminist movement we need to work harder to show parents the ways ending sexism positively changes family life. Feminist movement is pro-family. Ending patriarchal domination of children, by men or women, is the only way to make the family a place where children can be safe, where they can be free, where they can know love" – Bell Hooks, *Feminism is for Everybody: Passionate Politics*

Extracted from <www.goodreads.com/quotes/search?commit=Search&page=2&q=women+lack&utf8=%E2%9C%93>. Accessed on October 26, 2015.

**2.** In the text on page 27, the suffixes *-ment* and *-ance* were added to *empower* and *attend* to form *empowerment* and *attendance*.
These suffixes indicate

- a person or thing that does a certain action.
- an action or a result of an action.

**3.** Form nouns with the suffixes *-ment* and *-ance* based on the verbs below. Then look up their meanings in an English-English dictionary and complete the table in your notebook.

| Verb | Noun | Definition |
|---|---|---|
| guide | ♦ | ♦ |
| agree | ♦ | ♦ |
| accept | ♦ | ♦ |
| tolerate | ♦ | ♦ |
| develop | ♦ | ♦ |

Unit 2 Women in Power

# LANGUAGE IN CONTEXT

## Discourse Markers

**1.** Read the following extracts from the opinion article on page 27. Then choose the correct alternatives to complete the sentences below.

> "This is not **because** we do not have the best intentions in mind, **but** mostly **because** we are trying to reach too far **and** do not respect the principle that some policies should be best left to the member states **and** communities to decide."

> "We have marginalised communities across Europe that lack basic amenities **such as** running water, that lack proper housing and access to different kinds of services including quality education. The school attendance of marginalised Roma in Eastern European countries falls steeply after the age of 12 **or** 13."

a. The words in bold are used to show turns, ♦, organize, and control what we say or write.
  - qualify nouns
  - join ideas
  - describe actions

b. In the first extract, the words *because*, *but*, and *and* express, respectively, ♦, ♦, and ♦.
  - addition; conclusion; alternative
  - sequence; reason; exemplification
  - reason; contrast; addition

c. In the second extract, the words *such as* and *or* convey the idea of ♦ and ♦ respectively.
  - exemplification; alternative
  - cause; concession
  - addition; reason

d. Conjuncts, ♦, linking words, and other words or phrases used in writing and speaking to sign or mark discourse are considered discourse markers.
  - adjectives
  - articles
  - connectives

**2.** Look at this passage from the text *Women in Power and Decision-making*. Write P if the markers express Purpose, S if they indicate Sequence and E if they show Exemplification.

[…] The Beijing conference agreement, known as the Platform for Action, dubbed women in power and decision-making one of 12 critical areas of concern. It made two essential commitments to change. First ♦, it called for measures ensuring women's equal access to and full participation in power structures and decision-making. Political quotas or positive measures are examples of these. By reserving seats or candidacies for women, they have driven dramatic increases in the number of women leaders in some countries. Second ♦, the Platform urged steps to increase women's ability to participate. Training on leadership, public speaking and political campaigning, for instance ♦, grooms women to compete, win and be good leaders who can inspire others. […]

Extracted from <beijing20.unwomen.org/en/in-focus/decision-making>. Accessed on October 26, 2015.

3. The table below lists common discourse markers. Refer to the previous activities to complete it with their meanings.

**TIP**

O estudo dos marcadores discursivos vai ajudá-lo(a) a compreender melhor as relações entre as ideias de um texto.

| Meanings | Discourse Markers |
|---|---|
| ♦ | and; also; besides; moreover; in addition |
| ♦ | or; nor; whether; either; neither |
| ♦ | yet; but; however; on the other hand; conversely |
| ♦ | for instance; for example; particularly; such as |
| ♦ | as; because; due to; since |
| ♦ | first; second; next; after that; then; previously; finally |

For more Discourse Markers, go to Language Reference, pages 168 and 169.

4. Read the following excerpt from the text *Once we make this dream a reality...* and complete it with the discourse markers from the box.

> and (2x)   but   however   previously   such as

Michelle Bachelet was sworn-in for a second term as President of Chile in March 2014. ♦, she was the first Executive Director of UN Women, from its inception in 2010 until March 2013. A longstanding women's rights advocate, she has promoted gender equality ♦ empowerment of women throughout her distinguished political career, including as her country's first female President, between 2006 and 2010. In this editorial, she says nearly 20 years after the adoption of the Beijing Declaration and Platform for Action, we must recognize significant progress, ♦ challenges remain in terms of gender equality and equity.

The year 2014 marks a very significant step towards building a fairer world for men ♦ women. This year we begin a year-long celebration ahead of the 20th anniversary of the Beijing Declaration and Platform for Action in 2015. This platform provided the framework to help countries devise public policies to push gender equality forward. We can see substantial progress across different fields.

♦, the results are not good enough. There are many inequities and inequalities that we must conquer in political, economic and social realms. We still see serious inequalities in the area of women's participation in decision-making.

[…] Worldwide, women represent less than 10 per cent of Members of Parliament in 38 countries. These inequalities are more pronounced in regions ♦ the Middle East, North Africa and Asia. […]

Chilean President Michelle Bachelet waves after delivering the annual presidential message at the Congress in Valparaiso, Chile, on May 21, 2015.

Extracted from <beijing20.unwomen.org/en/news-and-events/stories/2014/6/michelle-bachelet>. Accessed on August 8, 2015.

Unit 2   Women in Power

**5.** Look at each of the illustrations below and find discourse markers. Then read the statements and decide which one best explains each illustration.

a.

b.

- Lorena couldn't see herself as a beautiful and sensual woman, but now she understands that her physical disability is no reason to accept stereotypes that the media creates for her.

- Lorena is portrayed negatively by the media. They say she is inferior and sensual, for instance. However, she knows she is more than just a stereotype and she'll do her best to be free.

- In addition to losing weight, Whitney also decided to do everything she loves like her other friends do.

- Whitney tried really hard to lose weight until she finally realized she doesn't need to be thin to be happy.

### WRAPPING UP

Discuss the quote below with a classmate. Then in your notebook, write three sentences promoting the image of women in your community. Include at least two discourse markers in your sentences. After that, share your ideas with the class. Any surprises?

"Gender equality is more than a goal in itself. It is a precondition for meeting the challenge of reducing poverty, promoting sustainable development and building good governance."

(Kofi Annan, Ghanaian former Secretary-General of the United Nations)

Extracted from <www.brainyquote.com/quotes/quotes/k/kofiannan401690.html>. Accessed on August 9, 2015.

# LISTENING COMPREHENSION

## Before Listening

**1.** You are going to listen to the message Michelle Bachelet recorded for the 100th anniversary of International Women's Day, when she was Executive Director of UN Women. Can you predict what the missing expressions are? Choose some of the expressions from the box to complete the transcript.

| | | | |
|---|---|---|---|
| collective vision | equal opportunities | first leader | political leadership |
| collective voice | equal pay | maternity leave | women's right |

Today, on this 100th anniversary of International Women's Day, we celebrate a century of progress, a century of women using their ♦ to organize for change.

It is very appropriate that at the same time, we are celebrating the creation of UN Women, an ambitious international commitment to accelerate the realization of women's rights and gender equality.

I am honoured to be the ♦ of this new United Nations organization.

**honoured** (UK)
**honored** (US)

Much has been achieved over 100 years. When the first International Women's Day took place, women could vote only in two countries. Today, that right is virtually universal and women have now been elected to lead Governments in every continent. Women are participating in the workforce in greater and greater numbers and 67 countries have laws mandating equal pay for men and women; 126 countries have guaranteed ♦.

As we see on our television screens every day, women and girls are mobilizing, alongside men and boys, to advance political freedoms worldwide. While the achievement of gender equality is closer than ever before, we still have far to go.

Our vision in UN Women is a world where men and women have ♦ and capacities and the principles of gender equality are embedded in the development, peace and security agendas.

Realizing this vision involves opening up spaces for women's ♦, as trade and peace negotiators, as heads of corporations; it involves freeing women from gender-based violence and convincing key policy makers that where women fully contribute to their economies and societies, the gains for everyone are greatly increased.

Evidence shows that where women have access to good education, good jobs, land and other assets, national growth and stability are enhanced, and we see lower maternal mortality, improved child nutrition, greater food security and less risk of HIV and AIDS. Men and women around the world who share this vision have a new global champion in UN Women to help make our ♦ a reality.

I am determined that UN Women will live up to the hopes of those who worked so hard to establish it, and will generate new energy, bringing together people from every country, society and community in a shared endeavour.

Happy International Women's Day!

Extracted from <www.unbrussels.org/component/content/article/41-reports/253-international-womens-day-video-message-by-un-women-executive-director-michelle-bachelet.html>. Accessed on October 25, 2015.

## Listening

 **2.** Now listen to her message and check if your predictions were correct.

## After Listening

As Executive Director of UN Women, what is Michelle Bachelet trying to do to help achieve gender equality? Explain.

> ### PRONUNCIATION PRACTICE
>
>  There are two *th* sounds in English. Listen to these words and pay attention to their pronunciation.
>
> > thing
> > the
>
> Listen to the words again and repeat. As you can see, *th* is voiceless in *thing* and voiced in *the*.
>
> Now listen to these words and identify the ones that are voiced.
> - anything
> - birth
> - health
> - than
> - thanks
> - that
> - there
> - this
> - growth

## SPEAKING

Discuss the following questions with the whole class.

✓ Are women's rights respected and protected nowadays? How?

✓ Do you believe that gender equality is precondition for advancing development? Why/Why not?

✓ Is Brazil on the way to gender equality? Justify your opinion.

# WRITING

In pairs, follow the steps below and write an opinion article.

## Planning your opinion article

- Choose a topic you would like to write about.
- Do some research and gather enough information to support your arguments and opinions.
- Take notes of all relevant facts.
- Choose appropriate language taking into account who the readers of your article will be.

## Writing and rewriting your text

- Come up with a catchy title.
- Refer back to activity 6 on page 29 and make sure to use the main characteristics of opinion articles.
- Write a draft in your notebook.
- Ask another pair of students to read your opinion article and give suggestions to improve it.
- Make all the necessary changes and write a clean copy on a separate sheet of paper.

### REFLECTING AND EVALUATING

Go back to your opinion article and make sure you paid enough attention to the following topics:

- ✓ Did you come up with a title that grabs your readers' attention?
- ✓ Does the topic relate to an ongoing debate?
- ✓ Is the first paragraph interesting enough to keep your audience reading?
- ✓ Have you included facts that support your point of view?

## After writing

- Exchange your article with other classmates. Which one is the most persuasive? Why?
- Additionally, you can publish the articles on the school website or make a mural, so everybody can read them.

# SELF-ASSESSMENT

Chegamos ao fim da unidade 2. Convidamos você a refletir sobre seu desempenho até aqui e a responder às questões propostas abaixo, escolhendo uma das seguintes opções:

> Sim.

> Preciso me preparar mais.

### Questões

- Você adquiriu repertório suficiente para discutir e posicionar-se criticamente sobre a igualdade de direitos entre homens e mulheres em diferentes sociedades?
- Você se sente capaz de expressar sua opinião em relação aos benefícios que uma nação pode ter se investir na educação da mulher?
- Você se considera apto a ler e compreender um artigo de opinião em língua inglesa e reconhecer as características principais inerentes ao gênero?
- Você reúne conhecimentos linguístico-discursivos suficientes para produzir um artigo de opinião em língua inglesa?
- Você se sente preparado para escutar trechos de discurso e compreender a ideia principal neles expressa?

### Refletindo sobre suas respostas

- Como você analisa a evolução do seu aprendizado em relação à unidade anterior?
- De que forma suas práticas de aprendizagem no decorrer desta unidade influenciaram suas respostas?
- O que você pode fazer para aprimorar ainda mais os conhecimentos adquiridos nesta unidade?
    a. Procurar conhecer mais sobre as conquistas das mulheres em diferentes sociedades, de que forma tais conquistas se deram e qual a repercussão disso nos locais em questão.
    b. Ler mais artigos de opinião para desenvolver melhor minha capacidade de análise crítica.
    c. Aprofundar meus conhecimentos de língua inglesa, usando recursos diversos, de forma que minha participação nas atividades seja mais ativa.
    d. Outros.

# Further Practice 1 – Units 1 & 2

**1.** Choose the best option to complete the advice letter and the corresponding reply.

## Dear Abby

**Loving Stepfather Teaches Wife How to Accept Gay Son**

DEAR ABBY: I am a 91-year-old reader with a story to tell. In 1958, I married a man every woman would have loved to have. ♦ was one of a kind. I had two boys from a previous marriage, and this wonderful man adopted ♦.

In 1963, before homosexuality was understood or openly accepted, I discovered that my oldest son was gay. I didn't take it well because of the way I was raised. In fact, I came unglued. My husband took ♦ in his arms and said, "Honey, he is no different today than he was yesterday."

The rest is a long story, but this wonderful man – a stepfather – gave acceptance to his son and taught ♦ to me. His words helped me to value my own son as the person he is. If his words can help some other parent, I am passing ♦ on.

EVER GRATEFUL MOTHER, SANTA ROSA, CALIF.

DEAR GRATEFUL MOTHER: ♦ married a wise and compassionate man, and I want to thank you for sharing an important message for other parents of lesbian, gay, bisexual, transgender, and questioning children.

Adapted from <www.uexpress.com/dearabby/2015/4/2/loving-stepfather-teaches-wife-how-to>.
Accessed on September 3, 2015.

a. He – me – they – it – you - You

b. He – them - me – it – them - You

c. You – them - me – it – them – He

**2.** Answer the following questions based on the advice letter and Abby's reply.

a. How old was the woman when she wrote the letter?

b. Now refer back to page 13 and reread the other advice letter written to Abby. Do Grateful Mother and Finally Met Someone write for the same reason? Explain.

**3.** Read the passage below and choose the poster which best relates to it.

My husband took me in his arms and said, "Honey, he is no different today than he was yesterday."

a.
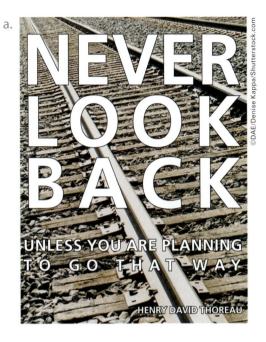

b.

**4.** Choose the best options to complete the sentences.

a. When Grateful Mother says that her husband is "one of a kind", she means that
- he is very similar to her first husband.
- he is a caring stepfather, but somewhat homophobic.
- he is a unique and very special man.

b. The decisive factors that made her change her mind were
- her husband's support and his wise words, full of love and understanding.
- the unconditional love and gratitude she felt for her family.
- her experience of a failed marriage and the fear of having a similar experience again.

c. Grateful Mother received from Abby
- an impartial reply.
- some advice as a reply.
- a thankful reply.

**5.** In pairs, discuss the questions below and write down the answers.

a. How did *Grateful Mother* deal with homosexuality back in 1963? Why was that? Which passage conveys her attitude towards homosexuality back then?

b. Do you think that most people would have the same attitude as the reader's second husband had? Why/Why not?

# Further Practice 1 – Units 1 & 2

**6.** Look at the posters from Migrant Workers Task Force (MWTF). Then choose the alternatives that apply to each poster.

Poster #1

Poster #2

Extracted from <https://mwtaskforce.wordpress.com/2011/04/26/antiracism-poster-campaign-for-labour-day-2011/>. Accessed on August 26, 2015

a. The short sentence at the top of the poster has a negative impact.

b. The negative impact is made positive by its complement.

c. It presents a rhetorical question to make readers reflect on it.

d. The whole poster presents a contrast.

e. The aim of the poster is to fight discrimination and prejudice.

**7.** Answer the questions based on the posters in activity 6.

a. Which personal characteristic does Lidya have that makes her strong enough to overcome discrimination?

b. What does she do on a daily basis to overcome discrimination?

c. How do you interpret the sentence "You see a housemaid, but she is a future ambassador of Lebanon to Ethiopia."?

d. What do you understand that "He is not worth a penny. He is worth gold." means?

**8.** Choose the best alternative to replace ♦ in the poem "She Walks in Beauty" by Lord Byron.

## She Walks in Beauty
by Lord Byron (Gerge Gordon)

She walks in beauty, like the night
Of cloudless climes ♦ starry skies;
♦ all that's best of dark and bright
Meet in her aspect and her eyes;
Thus mellow'd to that tender light
Which heaven to gaudy day denies.

One shade the more, one ray the less,
Had half impair'd the nameless grace
Which waves in every raven tress,
♦ softly lightens o'er her face;
Where thoughts serenely sweet express,
How pure, how dear their dwelling-place.

And on that cheek, and o'er that brow,
So soft, so calm, ♦ eloquent,
The smiles that win, the tints that glow,
♦ tell of days in goodness spent,
A mind at peace with all below,
A heart whose love is innocent!

WESTALL, Richard. *George Gordon Byron, 6th Baron Byron*. 1813. Oil on canvas. 36 in. × 28 in. (914 mm × 711 mm) National Portrait Gallery, London, England.

Extracted from <www.poetryfoundation.org/poem/173100>. Accessed on October 27, 2015.

a. and, Or, Or, but, Yet

b. and, And, Or, yet, But

c. or, But, But, yet, And

**9.** Read the poem again. Then answer the questions with YES or NO.

a. Is the woman identified by her name?

b. Does Lord Byron describe the woman's physical characteristics?

c. Has the woman made an impression on the poet?

d. Does the last stanza return to the woman's face?

# Further Practice 1 – Units 1 & 2

**10.** The poem *She Walks in Beauty* was written in the 19th century. How do you suppose women were regarded by society at that time? Is it different nowadays? How?

**11.** Read the cartoon and answer the questions.

"I'm a wife, a daughter, a working mother... and you're asking me if I can MULTI-TASK??"

    **a.** What do you understand by *multi-task*?

    **b.** Which context are the man and the woman in?

    **c.** What do you think the businessperson wanted to find out when he asked her if she could multi-task?

**12.** Now read this cartoon and compare it to the one in the previous activity. Then answer the question: What is the similarity between them?

" I juggle a family, a career, and three cell phones. "

# EXAM PRACTICE

As tiras compõem-se em geral de até quatro quadrinhos sequenciais. Elas, com frequência, apresentam comicidade e é comum que abordem temas econômicos, sociais e políticos.

Assinale a alternativa que melhor descreve a abordagem temática predominante nas tiras acima.

a. Embora as tiras apresentem certa comicidade, é evidente a predominância da reflexão política em ambos os contextos.

b. Em ambas as tiras, há quebra da expectativa do leitor no momento em que se lê o último quadro. A comicidade reside exatamente aí; contudo, a reflexão predominante é acerca da discriminação.

c. As abordagens temáticas são diferentes. Na tira *Peanuts*, a temática é infantil e, portanto, predominantemente centrada no humor. A tira *Grantland* apresenta um contexto de hierarquia profissional e, portanto, temática social.

d. Não há como identificar uma predominância temática nas tiras, uma vez que o sentido atribuído a elas dependerá exclusivamente da compreensão do leitor.

e. O contexto em ambas as tiras evidencia o aspecto econômico como temática predominante, pois podemos perceber a relação entre o opressor abastado e o oprimido.

# UNIT 3

# THEY CLAIM FOR RESPECT

Kayapo people from *Aldeia Moykarakô – Kaiapó-Mebengokré* Indigenous Territories, São Felix do Xingu, Pará, Brazil.

**Nesta unidade você terá oportunidade de:**

- refletir e discutir sobre a preservação dos direitos e da cultura indígena no Brasil e no mundo;
- reconhecer os objetivos e algumas das características das biografias e produzir uma;
- compreender uma reportagem sobre os jogos indígenas;
- fazer uma apresentação oral sobre aspectos culturais de tribos brasileiras.

- Onde a foto foi tirada?
- O que ela pode nos dizer sobre o lugar onde foi tirada?
- Que aspectos da cultura indígena estão retratados na foto?

# STARTING OUT

1. What do you see in these pictures? Which peoples do these elements originally associate with?

2. Below are some statements about Native Brazilian Tribes. Pick out the ones you think are true.

   a. There are about 240 tribes living in Brazil today.
   b. All Brazilian Indians live outside the Amazon.
   c. The largest Brazilian tribe is the Guarani.
   d. Malocas are big communal houses where some Indian tribes live.
   e. There are no uncontacted tribes in Brazil.

3. In pairs, answer the questions below. Then discuss your answers with the whole class.

   a. If you were looking for information about the lives of renowned personalities, what text genre would you read?
   b. Do you think biographies are good sources of information about these people?
   c. Do you like to read biographies? Why/Why not?
   d. Where can we usually find biographies?
   e. What kind of information do you think you can find in biographies?

# READING COMPREHENSION

## Before Reading

**1.** You are about to read Mário Juruna's biography. He was the first Brazilian indigenous federal representative. What do you think he fought for during his time in office?

## Reading

### Mário Juruna

Mário Juruna (Barra do Garças, September 3, 1942 or 1943 – Brasília, July 18, 2002) was the first national-level federal representative in Brazil that belonged to an indigenous people.

#### Biography

He was born in Namurunjá village, near Barra do Garças, in the state of Mato Grosso, the son of the Xavante *cacique* (chief) Apoenã. He lived in the jungle, without contact with civilization, until the age of 17, when he became *cacique*.

In the 1970s he became famous for walking the halls of FUNAI, in Brasilia to fight for land rights of Indians, while carrying a tape-recorder, which he used to record everything that was said to him and to prove that the authorities, in most cases, did not keep their word.

He was elected to the Chamber of Deputies of Brazil by the Democratic Labour Party from 1983-1987, representing Rio de Janeiro. His election had strong repercussions in Brazil and the world. He was responsible for the creation of a permanent commission for Indians, which brought formal recognition to issues related to Indians. In 1984, he denounced the businessman Calim Eid for having attempted to bribe him to vote for Paulo Maluf, the presidential candidate supported by the military regime then in power. He voted for Tancredo Neves, the democratic opposition candidate. He was not reelected in 1986, but he remained active in politics for several years. With his mandate ended, and abandoned by his tribe, he remained in Brasilia and died on July 18, 2002, due to complications from diabetes.

**labour** (UK)
**labor** (US)

Extracted from <www.worldheritage.org/articles/Mário_Juruna>. Accessed on August 11, 2015.

**2.** Identify the only sentence that is NOT true about Mário Juruna.

  **a.** His tribe was the Xavante.

  **b.** He wasn't reelected in 1986, so he abandoned politics.

  **c.** He was elected deputy to Brazil's lower house of Congress.

**3.** Match the events to their corresponding dates.

  Mário Juruna...

  **a.** became famous as an advocate for Native Brazilian rights.

  **b.** started his one and only political mandate.

  **c.** lost the elections.

  **d.** died.

  **e.** accused a businessperson of bribery.

  **1.** 2002   **3.** 1986   **5.** 1983

  **2.** 1970's   **4.** 1984

> **TIP**
> Buscar números, datas e imagens nos textos permite localizar informações específicas com mais rapidez e eficiência.

**4.** Answer the questions below.

  **a.** Were there any other Native Brazilian congresspeople in Brazil before Mário Juruna? Copy the part of the biography that justifies your answer.

  **b.** Why did he use to record what politicians said to him?

  **c.** What was he responsible for during his mandate?

**5.** Read the statements below and match them to the passages which prove they are correct. There is one extra passage.

  **a.** He was very young when he became *cacique*.

  **b.** He was a determined person who wanted to prove his point of view.

  **c.** Juruna wasn't an ambitious person looking for easy money.

  **d.** Even when he wasn't a deputy anymore, he was still interested in politics.

  **1.** In 1984, he denounced the businessman Calim Eid for having attempted to bribe him to vote for Paulo Maluf, the presidential candidate [...]

  **2.** He was not reeleted in 1986, but he remained active in politics for several years.

  **3.** He lived in the jungle, without contact with civilization, until the age of 17, when he became *cacique*.

  **4.** In the 1970s he became famous for walking the halls of Funai, in Brasilia, to fight for land rights of indians, while carrying a tape-recorder, which he used to record everything that was said to him and to prove that the authorities, in most cases, did not keep their word.

  **5.** He was born in Namurunjá village, near Barra do Garças, in the state of Mato Grosso, the son of the Xavante *cacique* (chief) Apoenã.

**6.** Read Juruna's quote below and look at his photograph on page 47 attentively. Then answer the question that follows.

> "*Eu nasci para morrer, eu nasci para brigar. Não nasci para ser expulso. Por que estou dentro do Brasil que é do índio. Eu nasci para isso.*"
>
> Extraído de <educacao.uol.com.br/biografias/mario-juruna.htm>. Acessado em: 25 de maio de 2016.

Do you think Juruna's photograph can illustrate the quote?

**7.** Read Sting's biography and reread Juruna's biography too. Then identify some characteristics you can recognize in them.

## Sting Biography

Gordon Matthew Thomas Sumner (born October 2, 1951), better known as Sting, is an English singer and musician. He first became famous as a member of the band The Police.

Sting was born in Newcastle, England in 1951 where he attended St. Cuthbert's Catholic High School. His father was a milkman in an area dominated by the ship building industry. From an early age, Sting displayed an aptitude and love for music, in particular the bass guitar. He sought to pursue a career in music, and took part in a variety of local gigs and gained some employment on cruises. [...]

His big break through came with the rock band Police. In 1978, he moved to London where, with Stewart Copeland and Andy Summers, they formed a group 'The Police'. They went onto sell many best-selling albums and won six Grammy awards. [...]

**Sting Activism and Charity**

His first solo performance came in 1981, when he performed in the fourth Amnesty International gala The Secret Policeman's Other Ball. He was a member of Band Aid (1984). In 1988, he founded the Rainforest foundation with his second wife Trudie Styler and Raoni Metuktire, a Kayapó Indian leader in Brazil. He is a member of Amnesty International, writing:

"I don't belong to a church or political party or a group of any kind. I feel that Amnesty International is the most civilized organization in history. Its currency is the written word. Its weapon is the letter; that's why I am a member. I believe in its non-violence; I believe in its effectiveness. Its dignity and its sense of commitment. Its focus on individuals and the concentration and tenacity with which they defend those imprisoned for their ideas has earned it the cautious respect of repressive governments throughout the world."

[...]

Extracted from <www.biographyonline.net/music/sting.html>. Accessed on May 26, 2016.

- **a.** They both present an accurate account of a person's life.
- **b.** They can present quotes.
- **c.** Both of them start at birth or early life.
- **d.** They do not mention how the person's life and legacy affect others.
- **e.** They highlight different aspects of their lifes.

**8.** Go back to Juruna's and Sting's biographies and find one more characteristic to add to the list given in the previous activity.

# After Reading

- What do you know about indigenous peoples around the world? Are their culture and rights preserved?
- Why is it important to preserve indigenous culture? Explain.
- Do you think that indigenous peoples should have more representation in the Brazilian Congress? Why?

# VOCABULARY STUDY

1. Read the extracts from the biography on page 47 and choose the alternatives that are close in meaning to the structures in bold.

   a. "[…] which he used to record everything that was said to him and to prove that the authorities, in most cases, did not **keep their word**."

   - air their opinion
   - do what they promised

   b. "In 1984, he denounced the businessman Calim Eid for having attempted to **bribe him** to vote for Paulo Maluf, […]"

   - use money to convince him
   - take him to court to convince him

   c. "[…] the presidential candidate **supported by** the military regime then in power."

   - tolerated by
   - backed up by

   d. "With his mandate ended, and abandoned by his tribe, he remained in Brasilia and died on July 18, 2002, **due to** complications from diabetes."

   - additionally
   - as a result of

2. Refer to the biography on page 47 to complete the word group table below with words related to the headings of each column. The first letter is given to help you out.

   | Locations | Politics | Occupations |
   |---|---|---|
   | v ♦ | m ♦ | c ♦ |
   | j ♦ | p ♦ | b ♦ |
   | h ♦ | r ♦ | d ♦ |

   > **TIP**
   > Lembre-se de que agrupar palavras por campo lexical (conjunto de palavras pertencentes à mesma área de conhecimento) é um recurso eficaz para o estudo e a ampliação do vocabulário.

3. Complete the captions below with some of the words from the table in activity 2.

a. Carlos Tukano has taken his fight from his remote ♦ to Rio's urban sprawl

b. Carlos Tukano is the son of the ♦ of the 5,000-strong Tukano tribe

Adapted from <www.bbc.com/news/world-latin-america-32195584>. Accessed on August 13, 2015.

# LANGUAGE IN CONTEXT

## Relative Pronouns

1. Read the following extracts from Mário Juruna's biography. Then read the statements that follow and write T (True) or F (False). Finally, correct the false ones.

   "Mário Juruna (Barra do Garças, September 3, 1942 or 1943 – Brasília, July 18, 2002) was the first national-level federal representative in Brazil **that** belonged to an indigenous people."

   "He lived in the jungle, without contact with civilization, until the age of 17, **when** he became *cacique*."

   "He was responsible for the creation of a permanent commission for Indians, **which** brought formal recognition to issues related to Indians."

   a. The words in bold are used to introduce additional information about an element that is about to come.

   b. *That*, *when*, and *which* refer to, respectively: the first national-level federal representative in Brazil, civilization, and a permanent commission for Indians.

   c. The relative pronoun we use depends on what we refer to.

2. Now read these extracts from the biography on page 47 and check the sentences that best explain them.

   a. "He voted for Tancredo Neves, the democratic opposition candidate."
   - Tancredo Neves, **who** voted for the opposition candidate, was the winner.
   - He voted for Tancredo Neves, **who** was the democratic opposition candidate.

   b. "In the 1970s he became famous for walking the halls of Funai, in Brasilia, to fight for land rights of Indians,"
   - The peoples **whose** land rights Juruna fought for were the Indians.
   - The lands **whose** rights Juruna fought for belonged to Funai.

   c. "He lived in the jungle, without contact with civilization, until the age of 17, when he became *cacique*."
   - Juruna lived in a jungle **where** he had no contact with civilization until the age of 17.
   - Juruna became *cacique* in a jungle **where** there was no contact with civilization for 17 years.

   d. "In 1984, he denounced the businessman Calim Eid for having attempted to bribe him to vote for Paulo Maluf, the presidential candidate supported by the military regime then in power."
   - Paulo Maluf denounced the businessman **that** supported the military regime.
   - In 1984, Juruna denounced the businessman **that** had attempted to bribe him.

They Claim for Respect   Unit 3

3. Refer to the previous activities and match the columns to form meaningful sentences.

   a. We use the relative pronoun *which*
   b. The relative pronoun *when* is used
   c. *That* is a relative pronoun used
   d. *Who* is a relative pronoun used

   - to refer to people, while *whose* refers to possession.
   - to refer to time and *where* is used to refer to places.
   - when we refer to things.
   - to refer to people and things.

4. Transform the two sentences below into one. Use the relative pronouns in parentheses and make all the necessary adjustments.

   a. The Guarani were one of the first peoples to have contact with Europeans in South America. They make up Brazil's most numerous tribe. (who)

   b. The Kaiowá, together with the Nandeva and the M'byá, are the three Guarani groups in Brazil. Kaiowá means "forest people". (which)

   c. Most communities have a religious leader. His authority is not based on formal power but on prestige. (whose)

   d. The Guarani share an everlasting desire to search for new lands. In the new lands there will be no pain and suffering. (where)

   e. In the last 500 years, nearly all the Guarani's land was taken from them. These lands are especially located in Mato Grosso do Sul. (which)

   f. The Guarani children starve. Their leaders have been assassinated. (whose)

A Guarani Indian playing the flute at Aracruz, Espírito Santo, Brazil.

Based on <www.survivalinternational.org/tribes/guarani>. Accessed on August 14, 2015.

## Prepositions of Time

**5.** Read the extracts and then complete the sentences.

"**In** the 1970s he became famous for walking the halls of FUNAI, [...]"

"**In** 1984, he denounced the businessman Calim Eid [...]"

"he remained in Brasilia and died **on** July 18, 2002, [...]"

a. We use ♦ before years and long periods of time.

b. We use ♦ before dates.

For more Prepositions of Time, refer to Language Reference, page 171.

**6.** Complete the news passages below with the correct preposition.

a. **First Amazon Indian to run London Marathon**
20 April 2015

Nixiwaka Yawanawá will be the first Amazon Indian to run the London Marathon ♦ Sunday, April 26, 2015.

Nixiwaka is raising vital funds for Survival International — the global movement for tribal peoples' rights — together with Survival's co-founder and President Robin Hanbury-Tenison, who is running the marathon as one of eight challenges to mark his 80th year.
[...]

Extracted from <www.survivalinternational.org/news/10740>. Accessed on August 14, 2015.

Nixiwaka Yamanawá training for the London Marathon ♦ April 2015.

b. **Brazil: Gunmen set fire to Indian community**
26 June 2015

*Kalapalo* Indigenous Tribe, *Aldeia Aiha*. Xingu Indigenous Park, Mato Grosso, 2011.

Gunmen have attacked and set ablaze a Guarani Indian community in southwest Brazil.
Initial reports indicated that a one-year-old baby had burned to death when the gunmen torched the Indians' houses ♦ June 24, but this has not subsequently been confirmed.
[...]

Adapted from <www.survivalinternational.org/news/10832>. Accessed on August 14, 2015.

### WRAPPING UP

In pairs, write sentences with the elements listed below using relative pronouns. If necessary, refer back to the texts you have read in this unit to recall what the words refer to. Then read your sentences to the class. Are they similar?

Namurunjá          Apoenã          The Guarani

They Claim for Respect   Unit 3   53

# LISTENING COMPREHENSION

## Before Listening

1. You are about to listen to a TV news report from Al Jazeera about the 2013 edition of the Indigenous Games. The pictures below represent some of the sports included in these games. Look and check the ones you expect to find in such a competition. Use a dictionary to help you name these sports.

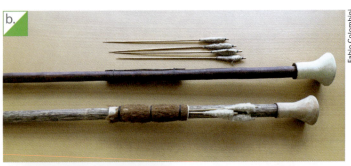

**football** (UK)
**soccer** (USA)

## Listening

2. Listen to the TV news report and answer the questions. Then refer to the transcript on page 183 to check your answers.

   a. Which edition of the Indigenous Games is mentioned?

   b. Where did the games take place?

   c. Among all the sports they compete in, which one is not traditional?

   d. According to the journalist, what makes the Indigenous Games more special than the World Cup and the Olympic Games?

**3.** Listen to the TV news report again and choose the only sentence you cannot infer.

   **a.** Many tribes take part in the games because they believe it is a way to share indigenous culture with the outside world.

   **b.** Most of the indigenous people are extremely competitive.

   **c.** The participants live the games intensely.

**4.** In your notebook, write the missing information.

   **a.** Name of the reporter: ♦

   **b.** Place the reporter was when he presented the news: ♦

## After Listening

Do you think that the Indigenous Games help to preserve indigenous culture? Justify.

### PRONUNCIATION PRACTICE

Word stress is important in speaking and understanding English. Listen to these words and pay attention to their stress.

| **wres**tling | in**dig**enous | compe**ti**tion |

Now listen to these words and find out to which column they belong.

| ceremonial | champion | integrate |
| participate | previous | traditional |

| **wres**tling | in**dig**enous | compe**ti**tion |

# SPEAKING

In small groups, prepare a picture-based slide presentation about any other aspect of the Brazilian indigenous culture.

✓ Choose a Brazilian indigenous tribe and do some research about it in magazines, books, or on the Internet.

✓ Look for information related to the tribe's culture.

✓ Decide on only one aspect to share with the whole group. Choose three or four pictures that illustrate that topic.

✓ Show the pictures to your teacher and tell him/her what you want to talk about.

✓ Present the slides to your classmates.

# WRITING

In pairs, follow the steps below and write a biography.

## Planning the biography

- Exchange ideas with your classmate on some people you both admire.
- Choose a person you are interested in learning more about.
- Do some research about him/her on the Internet or in books.
- Think about the questions below before selecting information:
  – What made or still makes this person so special?
  – How does he/she influence people?
  – Were there any events that changed his/her life?
  – Did he/she overcome obstacles? What kind of obstacles were they?
  – In your notebook, take notes about important dates and facts of his/her life.

## Writing and rewriting your text

- Organize your notes and refer back to activity 7 on page 49 to review some characteristics of biographies.
- Write a draft in your notebook
- Ask your teacher to correct it. Then make all the necessary changes.
- Write a final version on a sheet of paper and add a photograph of the person.

> **REFLECTING AND EVALUATING**
>
> Go back to your draft and make sure you paid attention to the following topics:
> ✓ Is your biography organized chronologically?
> ✓ Have you included relevant facts?
> ✓ Are there verbs in the past tense?

## After writing

- Create a biography book to be kept in the school library.
- Put all the biographies together and create a book cover with your classmates.
- Alternatively, publish the biography you have written on the school website or in the school newspaper.

# SELF-ASSESSMENT

Chegamos ao fim da unidade 3. Convidamos você a refletir sobre seu desempenho até aqui e responder às questões propostas abaixo, escolhendo uma das seguintes opções:

- Sim.
- Preciso me preparar mais.

### Questões

- Você tem conhecimento suficiente para expor sua opinião acerca da preservação dos direitos e da cultura indígena no Brasil e no mundo?
- Você se sente capaz de ler e compreender biografias em língua inglesa e reconhecer as características principais inerentes ao gênero?
- Você reúne conhecimentos linguístico-discursivos suficientes para redigir uma biografia em língua inglesa?
- Você está preparado para escutar reportagens sobre os jogos indígenas e compreender informações específicas?
- Você se julga apto a fazer uma apresentação sobre uma tribo indígena brasileira?

### Refletindo sobre suas respostas

- Como você analisa a evolução do seu aprendizado em relação à unidade anterior?
- De que forma suas práticas de aprendizagem no decorrer desta unidade influenciaram em suas respostas?
- O que você pode fazer para aprimorar ainda mais os conhecimentos adquiridos nesta unidade?

   a. Buscar por mais informações sobre a influência e preservação da cultura indígena no mundo, bem como sobre a presença indígena em diferentes setores da sociedade atual.

   b. Ler biografias de representantes indígenas que tenham lutado pela preservação da cultura indígena ou de outras personalidades que tenham lutado por uma causa social de relevância para a preservação da cultura de uma nação.

   c. Aprofundar meus conhecimentos em língua inglesa, usando recursos diversos, de forma que minha participação nas atividades seja mais ativa.

   d. Outros.

# UNIT 4

# WHAT DOES FRIENDSHIP MEAN TO YOU?

**Nesta unidade você terá oportunidade de:**

- refletir e discutir sobre o valor da amizade;
- reconhecer algumas das características das letras de música e escrever uma;
- compreender um *podcast* sobre relações de amizade;
- compartilhar com a turma suas experiências de amizade.

- Quais os elementos em evidência na imagem?
- Que relação podemos estabelecer entre esses elementos e o título da unidade?

# STARTING OUT

1. Read the posters and answer the question: What do they show?

a. Wherever you are it is your friends who make your world.

b. Who finds a faithful friend finds a treasure.

2. Choose the words you associate with friendship.

- ambition
- animosity
- caring
- companionship
- dedication
- disregard
- neglect
- solidarity
- trust
- understanding

3. What other text genres besides posters are often employed to promote the value of friendship? Talk to your classmate and write down your ideas in your notebook. Then share your thoughts with the class. Did you come up with similar ideas?

60  Unit 4  What Does Friendship Mean to You?

# READING COMPREHENSION

## Before Reading

**1.** Look at the structure of the text and the picture below. Then answer: what text genre is it? Do you know who the people in the picture are?

## Reading

### You're My Best Friend

(John Deacon)

Ooh you make me live
Whatever this world can give to me
It's you you're all I see
Ooh you make me live now honey
Ooh you make me live

Ooh you're the best friend that I ever had
I've been with you such a long time
You're my sunshine and I want you to know
That my feelings are true
I really love you
Oh you're my best friend

Ooh you make me live

Ooh I've been wandering round
But I still come back to you
In rain or shine
You've stood by me girl
I'm happy at home
You're my best friend

Ooh you make me live
Whenever this world is cruel to me
I got you to help me forgive
Ooh you make me live now honey
Ooh you make me live

You're the first one
When things turn out bad
You know I'll never be lonely
You're my only one
And I love the things
I really love the things that you do
Ooh you're my best friend

Ooh you make me live
I'm happy at home
You're my best friend
Oh, oh you're my best friend
Ooh you make me live
You're my best friend

A música *You're My Best Friend*, interpretada pela banda inglesa de *rock* Queen, encontra-se no álbum *A Night at the Opera*. A letra e a música foram escritas por John Deacon.

Extracted from <www.metrolyrics.com/youre-my-best-friend-lyrics-queen.html>. Accessed on October 26, 2015.

The hard rock band *Queen*.

### TIP

Ouvir músicas em inglês é um excelente exercício para adquirir vocabulário, conhecer expressões contextualizadas, aprimorar a habilidade de compreensão auditiva e praticar pronúncia. Procure conhecer as letras das músicas de que você mais gosta e aprenda enquanto se diverte.

2. Choose the best answers to the questions below.

   a. Which quote best expresses the theme of *You're My Best Friend*?

   1. "You don't choose your family. They are God's gift to you, as you are to them." (Desmond Tutu, South African activist)
   2. "Love is composed of a single soul inhabiting two bodies." (Aristotle, Greek Philosopher)
   3. "One of the most beautiful qualities of true friendship is to understand and to be understood." (Lucius Annaeus Seneca, Roman Philosopher)

   Extracted from <www.brainyquote.com/>. Accessed on August 13, 2015.

   b. Which verse shows that the friends have been together for a long time?

   - # 1
   - # 2
   - # 4

3. Read the definition of metaphor and, in pairs, explain the meaning of the following passage: "You're my sunshine and I want you to know / That my feelings are true."

   > **Metaphor** a word or phrase for one thing that is used to refer to another thing in order to show or suggest that they are similar

   Extracted from <www.merriam-webster.com/dictionary/metaphor>. Accessed on August 13, 2015.

4. Match the song titles to the verses of two songs. Then answer the question: which of them moves you the most?

   a. Gift of a Friend    b. See You Again

   **1**

   **Wiz Khalifa and Charlie Puth**

   How can we not talk about family
   When family's all that we got?
   Everything I went through
   You were standing there by my side
   And now you gon' be with me for the last ride

   Extracted from <www.azlyrics.com/lyrics/wizkhalifa/seeyouagain.html>. Accessed on October 27, 2015.

   **2**

   **Demi Lovato**

   Someone who knows when you're lost and you're scared
   There through the highs and the lows
   Someone to count on, someone who cares
   Beside you wherever you go

   Extracted from <www.azlyrics.com/lyrics/demilovato/giftofafriend.html>. Accessed on October 27, 2015.

5. Read the lyrics of *Canção da América*. Then consider its structure and theme and answer the question: what are the similarities between this song and the one on page 61?

### Canção da América
(Milton Nascimento e Fernando Brant)

Amigo é coisa para se guardar
Debaixo de sete chaves
Dentro do coração
Assim falava a canção que na América ouvi
Mas quem cantava chorou
Ao ver o seu amigo partir

Mas quem ficou, no pensamento voou
Com seu canto que o outro lembrou
E quem voou, no pensamento ficou
Com a lembrança que o outro cantou

Amigo é coisa para se guardar
No lado esquerdo do peito
Mesmo que o tempo e a distância digam "não"
Mesmo esquecendo a canção
O que importa é ouvir
A voz que vem do coração

Pois seja o que vier, venha o que vier
Qualquer dia, amigo, eu volto
A te encontrar
Qualquer dia, amigo, a gente vai se encontrar

Canção da América. Milton Nascimento / Fernando Brant © 1994 by NASCIMENTO EDIÇÕES MUSICAIS LTDA / 3 PONTAS (DUBAS). Accessed on October 28, 2015.

Milton Nascimento was a special local guest at the Amnesty International "Human Rights Now!" world tour stop in São Paulo, Brazil.

6. Read the lyrics of the song *Canção da América* again and pay attention to the words that rhyme. Then discuss the questions with a classmate: do the song lyrics on page 62 rhyme? In your opinion, why is rhyming so common in song lyrics?

## After Reading

- What is the role of digital technology and social media in friendships?
- In your opinion, what makes a good friend? Explain.
- Have you ever hurt a friend? If so, what did you do? If not, what would you do if you hurt a friend?

# VOCABULARY STUDY

1. Refer to the song *You're My Best Friend* to infer the meanings of the extracts below. Then choose the alternative which best explains them.

   a. "I've been wandering round"
      - I've walked aimlessly
      - I've searched for you everywhere

   b. "You've stood by me girl"
      - You failed to back me up
      - You were there when I needed you

   c. When things turn out bad
      - When good things overcome the bad ones
      - When things end up being bad

2. In your notebook, match the definitions about relationships in the box to the phrasal verbs (a-f) below.

   > to admire and respect someone
   >
   > to argue with someone and stop being friendly with them
   >
   > to be attracted to someone and start to love that person
   >
   > to end or cause something to end, esp. a personal or business relationship
   >
   > to forgive someone and be friendly with them again after an argument or disagreement
   >
   > to make someone feel foolish and unimportant

   Extracted from <dictionary.cambridge.org/dictionary/english/>. Accessed on October 26, 2015.

   a. look up to someone
   b. fall out
   c. make up
   d. break up (something)
   e. fall for (someone)
   f. put down (someone)

3. Match the columns to form famous proverbs about friendship. Then talk to a classmate about whether or not you agree with them.

   a. A friend cannot be known in prosperity;
   b. A friend is one who knows you
   c. A friend that isn't in need
   d. A friend will joyfully sing with you when you are on the mountain top,

      - is a friend indeed.
      - and loves you just the same.
      - and silently walk beside you through the valley.
      - an enemy cannot be hidden in adversity.

   Extracted from <www.proverb.taiwanonline.org/display.php?thm=true&actual=Friendship&term=friend&row=0>. Accessed on October 26, 2015.

# LANGUAGE IN CONTEXT

## Present Perfect I

1. Read these extracts from the lyrics on page 61 and pay attention to the verb forms in bold. Then choose the correct alternatives to complete the sentences.

> "You're the best friend
> That I ever had
> **I've been** with you such a long time
> You're my sunshine and I want you to know
> That my feelings are true
> I really love you
> You're my best friend"
>
> [...] I've been wandering round
> But I still come back to you
> In rain or shine
> You**'ve stood** by me girl
> I'm happy at home
> You're my best friend"

**Contracted form**
have = 've

a. The highlighted verb forms are actions that *started and finished at a specific time in the past / started at an unspecific time in the past and continue up to the present*.

b. The Present Perfect tense is formed by *have* (or *has*) + past participle of the *main / auxiliary* verb.

For more information about the Present Perfect tense, refer to Language Reference, pages 173 and 174. For irregular past participles, refer to the Irregular Verbs List, page 189.

2. Identify the correct alternative to complete the text below.

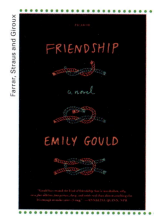

**A novel about two friends learning the difference between getting older and growing up**

Bev Tunney and Amy Schein ♦ best friends for years; now, at thirty, they're at a crossroads. Bev is a Midwestern striver still mourning a years-old romantic catastrophe. Amy is an East Coast princess whose luck and charm ♦ too long ♦ her to cruise through life. [...]

Extracted from <www.goodreads.com/book/show/18490619-friendship?from_search=true&search_version=service>. Accessed on August 16, 2015.

- has been / hasn't... allowed
- have been / have... allowed
- were / has... allowed

What Does Friendship Mean to You? **Unit 4**  65

**3.** Here are some verses from songs about friendship. Use the contracted form of the Present Perfect to complete them with the verbs from the box.

be   grow   know

**a.**
I'll be there for you
When the rain starts to pour
I'll be there for you
Like I ♦ there before
I'll be there for you
Cause you're there for me too...

(*I'll Be There For You*, The Rembrandts)

Extracted from <www.azlyrics.com/lyrics/rembrandts/illbethereforyouthemefromfriends.html>. Accessed on August 12, 2015.

**b.**

Thank you for all of your trust
Thank you for not giving up
Thank you for holding my hand
I ♦ always ♦ where you stand

(*Best Friend*, Jason Mraz)

Extracted from <www.azlyrics.com/lyrics/jasonmraz/bestfriend.html>. Accessed on August 16, 2015.

**c.**
I'll never let another get that close to me
You see I ♦ a lot smarter now
Sometimes you have to choose and then you'll see
If your friend is true they'll be there with you
Through the thick and thin

(*What About Your Friends*, TLC)

Extracted from <www.vagalume.com.br/tlc/what-about-your-friends.html>. Accessed on August 27, 2015.

## Present Perfect and Simple Past

**4.** Now read a few more lines of the song *I'll Be There For You*. Identify the verb form indicating an action that happened at a definite past time, and then the verb form indicating an action that happened at an indefinite past time.

"You're still in bed at ten
And work began at eight
You've burned your breakfast
So far... Things are going great"

**5.** Based on the lines in activity 4, complete the sentences below with *Simple Past* or *Present Perfect*.

  **a.** We often use the ♦ to talk about actions that happened at unspecified times in the past, actions that started in the past and have a consequence in the present or continue up to the present, or for actions that have happened up to now.

  **b.** We often use the ♦ for actions that started and finished in the past, actions that happened at definite times in the past, and actions as part of a list of complete actions in the past.

**6.** Complete the following advice letters with the verbs in parentheses. Use the Simple Past or the Present Perfect.

  **a.** I think I ♦ really ♦ (hurt) several people's feelings. Yesterday I ♦ (say) something insensitive to Friend A about Friend B and Friend C, and I don't think any of them will like me now. I feel really guilty. What should I do please?
  — Elizabeth*

  No one's perfect. We all mess up now and then and wish we could hit some magical "undo" key. It can help a little bit to remember that most people ♦ (be) in the situation you're in. What makes the difference is what you do next.

  [...]

  Extracted from &lt;kidshealth.org/teen/expert/friends/apologize.html&gt;. Accessed on August 16, 2015.

  **b.** I ♦ (fall out) with my friend. What can I do?

  Sometimes friends fall out. Usually they make up again soon, but sometimes the arguments are more serious. These can feel terrible. People who were part of your life are suddenly not there. Try talking to your friend and explaining how you feel.

  If you ♦ (hurt) them, be prepared to say sorry and find a way to make it better.

  [...]

  Extracted from &lt;www.childline.org.uk/Explore/Friends/Pages/Friendships.aspx&gt;. Accessed on August 16, 2015.

## WRAPPING UP

In pairs, describe the picture. Then answer the questions that follow. Finally, share your answers with the class.

What qualities do you look for in a friend?

What kinds of things have your friends done to prove they're really your friends?

Have you ever lost good friends? What happened?

What Does Friendship Mean to You? **Unit 4**

# LISTENING COMPREHENSION

## Before Listening

**1.** In pairs, read the comic strip and answer: what does Chuck's sister mean when she says, "No, but I know my brother."?

Extracted from: <www.peanuts.com/search/?pubdate=&sort_by=bydate&seanonal=&stardate=&enddate=&character%5B%5D=Marcie&select character=%27Marcie%27 keyword=friend&type=comic _strips#.VxZQq_krKm_>. Accessed on May 12, 2016.

## Listening

**2.** Before you listen to the first part of a podcast about friendship, read the first three paragraphs and put them in order. Then listen and check your answers.

> *Podcast* é uma combinação das palavras *iPod* e *broadcasting*.
>
> Baseado em: <computer.howstuffworks.com/internet/basics/podcasting.htm>. Acessado em: 26 de outubro de 2015.

♦ Now, you would think going to Rome would be exciting enough, and of course it is, even though I've been [there] many, many times. I'm so fortunate to have a lot of family there. To me, going to Rome, on this occasion, is about so much more than the beautiful, the magical, the stunning city of Rome with which I am absolutely head over heels in love. For me, going to Rome this time marks a special occasion.

♦ As I'm recording this podcast, I'm ridiculously excited, elated, exhilarated even, because this evening, I am driving a couple of hours to go and see a very good friend of mine, Claire, who lives very close to Manchester airport, which is very handy on this occasion, because I am going to spend a few hours with her this evening, crash at her house, and sneak out before dawn to catch an early morning flight to Rome.

♦ Hello again, and welcome to another happiness podcast with me, Frederika Roberts, the happiness speaker. Today, I want to talk to you about friendship, and the importance of friendship.

68  Unit 4  What Does Friendship Mean to You?

**3.** Listen to the second part of the podcast and choose the correct answers.

> *Err*, assim como *um*, *uh*, *like*, *you know* e outras expressões semelhantes, é considerado um *filler*. Os *fillers* são frequentemente usados na linguagem oral para dar tempo aos falantes para pensar no que vão dizer em seguida.

a. How does the speaker feel when she meets her old friends?
- She feels like they are 23 years back in time. It's like no time has elapsed.
- She feels like they don't have much in common anymore, but they are still friends.

b. How often does Frederika go to Luxembourg to visit her old friends?
- Every Christmas.
- Every couple of years.

c. Who does she refer to when she says, "We're there for each other no matter what"?
- Claire from Manchester and Nadège from Germany.
- Claire from Brussels and Nadège from Germany.

d. What do Frederika, Claire and Nadège do so they can spend a little more time together?
- They get together in a flat for a whole weekend in Rome.
- Frederika flies to Brussels with Claire and they meet Nadège there.

## After Listening

What do you think of Frederika's feelings towards her two friends? Explain your answer in your notebook.

# SPEAKING

In small groups, talk about friendship and your personal friendship experiences. Use the questions below to guide the conversation.

How important is friendship to you?

Do you have any friends from your childhood? If so, how do you keep in touch with them? If not, why?

Which qualities do you like the most in your friends? What do you like the least?

How do you deal with your friends' negative characteristics?

Do your friends trust in you?

Have you and your friends ever had an amazing adventure? What did you do and what was it like?

Now choose a person from your group to report your conversation to the whole class.

# WRITING

In small groups, write your own song lyrics.

## Planning the lyrics

- Talk to your classmate and decide on a topic. Here are some suggestions:

    You can write about…
    - what inspires or upsets you.
    - a person you like.
    - something that has changed your life.
    - a very special friend or family member.

- Look for inspiration in your favorite songs.

## Writing and rewriting your text

- Write a draft in your notebook.
- Don't forget that successful lyrics get stuck in people's minds mostly because they reflect common experiences that everyone has had.
- Revise your draft and ask the teacher to correct it.
- Write a clean copy on a sheet of paper.

### REFLECTING AND EVALUATING

Go back to your lyrics and make sure you paid enought attention to the following topics:
- ✓ Is the title catchy?
- ✓ Is the story organized in verses?
- ✓ Does it rhyme?
- ✓ Do you think it will connect with people?

## After writing

- Present the lyrics you have written to the whole class. You can read the words aloud or sing them, if you wish.
- Vote for the most creative lyrics.

# SELF-ASSESSMENT

Chegamos ao fim da unidade 4. Convidamos você a refletir sobre seu desempenho até aqui e responder às questões propostas abaixo, escolhendo uma das seguintes opções:

Sim.   Preciso me preparar mais.

### Questões

- Você reúne argumentos suficientes para expor, de maneira clara e coerente, sua opinião em relação ao valor da amizade, bem como para relatar algumas de suas experiências pessoais em diferentes períodos da sua vida?
- Você está apto a ler e compreender diferentes letras de música e reconhecer as características principais inerentes ao gênero?
- Você reúne conhecimentos linguístico-discursivos para criar uma letra de música?
- Você está preparado para escutar *podcasts* sobre amizade e compreender as relações neles descritos?

### Refletindo sobre suas respostas

- Como você analisa a evolução do seu aprendizado em relação à unidade anterior?
- De que forma suas práticas de aprendizagem no decorrer desta unidade influenciaram suas respostas?
- O que você pode fazer para aprimorar ainda mais os conhecimentos adquiridos nesta unidade?
    a. Buscar por mais informações acerca do comportamento das pessoas em relação à amizade no mundo contemporâneo, bem como sobre as expectativas e receios a respeito dessas relações.
    b. Ler letras de música em língua inglesa para ampliar meu vocabulário e observar as estruturas linguísticas comumente usadas nesse gênero textual.
    c. Aprofundar meus conhecimentos em língua inglesa, usando recursos diversos, de forma que minha participação nas atividades seja mais ativa.
    d. Outros.

# Further Practice 2 – Units 3 & 4

**1.** Read the text below and answer the questions.

### Interview with Megaron Txucarramãe (2005)

Interview with Megaron Txucarramãe, conducted at the Hemispheric Institute's 5th Encuentro titled *Performing Heritage: Contemporary Indigenous and Community-Based Practices* which took place in Belo Horizonte, Brazil, in 2005. In this interview he talks about Kaiapó cultural practices and traditions, as well as their current situation in contemporary Brazilian geopolitics. He also comments on his people's participation in the Encuentro, where Megaron also delivered a keynote address titled *The Indigenous Question* in Brazil.

#### Biography

**Megaron Txucarramãe** (leader of the Mebêngôkre/Kaiapó) is one of the most important native leaders in Brazil, with outstanding performance on behalf of his people, Mekragnotire, and of other Brazilian native people. Working at FUNAI, he acted in Contact Fronts of the Ikpeng and Panará People. In 1984 he took part in the setting of the land boundaries of the Native Land Kapôt-Jarina and, in 1992/1993, of the Native Land Mekragnotire. He was a FUNAI supervisor of the Parque Indígena do Xingu (Xingu Indians Park) from 1984 to 1994 and was the director of FUNAI-Colíder/MT from 1995-2011. He is also a founder member of the Associação Ipren-re de Defesa do Povo Mebêngôkre (Ipren-re Association for the Mebêngôkre People) in 1993.

Adapted from <hemi.nyu.edu/hemi/fr/enc05-interviews/item/1806-interview-with-megaron-txucaramãe>. Accessed on August 26, 2015.

a. What was the interview about?

b. How long was Megaron Txucarramãe director of FUNAI?

c. What else did he do at FUNAI?

d. What can you infer about his work for Brazil's indigenous people? Justify your answer.

**2.** Read the quote below and answer the question: why is the wisdom of the ancient indigenous people important for us?

> Through consciousness, our minds have the power to change our planet and ourselves. It is time we heed the wisdom of the ancient indigenous people and channel our consciousness and spirit to tend the garden and not destroy it.
>
> (Bruce Lipton, American Biologist)

Extracted from <www.brainyquote.com/quotes/keywords/indigenous.html>. Accessed on May 26, 2016.

**3.** Choose the best alternative to complete the text.

### Amazon tribal chief's SOS: the white man is destroying everything

Leader who enlisted Sting to save rainforest tells Tom Bawden the problem is as bad as ever

TOM BAWDEN
Tuesday 10 June 2014

The Brazilian tribal leader ♦ enlisted Sting to help save the Amazon rainforest has accused the developed world of being intent on "destroying everything" and urged its citizens to fundamentally change the way they think.

Twenty-five years ago, Chief Raoni Metuktire, of the indigenous Kayapo population, shot to international prominence as his campaign against hydroelectric dams on the Xingu river galvanized The Police's frontman.

With the help of Sting and his wife, Trudie Styler, Chief Raoni generated so much publicity he was able to defeat a series of proposed dams along the Xingu, a major tributary of the Amazon ♦ this tribe lives, in the early 1990s.

But the threat has resurfaced, and at a far greater magnitude, with proposals to build up to 60 hydroelectric dams now at various stages of development across the Amazon, including at least six on the Xingu.

Speaking to The Independent through a translator, Chief Raoni, said: "The white man seems to be destroying everything. Try to change the way you think and tell your children ♦ they're growing up that it's very important to respect nature, to respect indigenous peoples, and not to destroy everything, not to finish everything.

"All over the world indigenous people are having problems with the destruction of their land and forest. Everywhere I look there is occupation and destruction of the natural balance.

"We should be finding a solution together to preserve the forest for the future of our children and our grandchildren and our great-grandchildren. What's going to happen when it's all gone, when it's all destroyed and there's nothing left?"

The Kayapo population numbers about 8,500, most of them living in a handful of villages in the eastern part of the rainforest.

[...]

Kayapo Indian Chief Raoni Metuktire from Aldeia Piaruçu. Capoto Indigenous Territories, Jarina São José do Xingu, Mato Grosso, 2011.

Extracted from <www.independent.co.uk/environment/green-living/amazon-tribal-chiefs-sos-the-white-man-is-destroying-everything-9524549.html>. Accessed on August 25, 2015.

**a.** when, where, who

**b.** who, where, who

**c.** who, where, while

# Further Practice 2 – Units 3 & 4

4. What do you think about celebrities who are engaged in social causes? Do you think they can make a difference? Share your point of view.

5. The picture below is a reproduction of Tarsila do Amaral's painting *Baptism of Macunaíma* (1956). Look at the painting and identify the sentences you can infer.

AMARAL, Tarsila. *Baptism of Macunaíma*. 1956. Oil on canvas. 132,5 x 250 cm.

   a. The baby in the woman's hands is Macunaíma.

   b. The baby was probably born in an indigenous tribe.

   c. The Native Brazilians of the tribe are not interested in Macunaíma's baptism.

   d. The work was based on Mário de Andrade's novel *Macunaíma*.

6. What other aspects of the painting are meaningful to you?

7. Do some research or talk to your literature teacher to answer the questions below.
   Do you know any other books or poems from Brazilian literature whose main characters are indigenous? What are they about?

8. Read the lyrics of *Count On Me* by the American singer and composer Bruno Mars. Then complete the text using the expressions from the box.

> And I know when I need it
> friends are supposed to do, oh yeah
> how much you really mean to me
> I'll sail the world to find you
> my shoulder when you cry

## Count On Me

[Verse 1]
Oh uh-huh
If you ever find yourself stuck in the middle of the sea
♦
If you ever find yourself lost in the dark and you can't see
I'll be the light to guide you

We find out what we're made of
When we are called to help our friends in need

[Chorus]
You can count on me like 1, 2, 3
I'll be there
♦
I can count on you like 4, 3, 2
And you'll be there
'Cause that's what friends are supposed to do, oh yeah
Ooooooh, oooohhh yeah, yeah

[Verse 2]
If you're tossin' and you're turnin'
And you just can't fall asleep
I'll sing a song beside you
And if you ever forget ♦
Every day I will remind you

Oooh
We find out what we're made of
When we are called to help our friends in need

[Chorus]
You can count on me like 1, 2, 3
I'll be there
And I know when I need it
I can count on you like 4, 3, 2
And you'll be there
'Cause that's what ♦
Ooooooh, oooohhh yeah, yeah

You'll always have ♦
I'll never let go, never say goodbye
You know...

[Chorus]
You can count on me like 1, 2, 3
I'll be there
And I know when I need it
I can count on you like 4, 3, 2
And you'll be there
'Cause that's what friends are supposed to do, oh yeah
Ooooooh, oooohhh

You can count on me 'cause I can count on you

Count on me
Autor: LAWRENCE, Philip Martin ii (ca)/ Levine, Ari(ca)/ Mars, Bruno (ca) editora : Warner Chappell Edições Musicais Ltda. Todos os direitos reservados

# Further Practice 2 – Units 3 & 4

**9.** Choose the best answer to the question.

What does this song have in common with the one on page 61?

a. It has the same number of verses and it is in a techno style.

b. It is organized in verses and focuses on friendship.

c. It has nothing in common with the song on page 61.

**10. Read the quotes below and identify the correct options to complete them.**

> "The friend in my adversity I shall always cherish most. I can better trust those who **helped / has helped** to relieve the gloom of my dark hours than those who are so ready to enjoy with me the sunshine of my prosperity."
> (Ulysses S. Grant, 18th President of the United States)

Extracted from <www.brainyquote.com/quotes/topics/topic_friendship2.html#1p078EF12swk5ebX.99>. Accessed on September 2, 2015.

> "You can always tell a real friend: when you **made / have made** a fool of yourself he doesn't feel you'**ve done / did** a permanent job."
> (Laurence J. Peter, Canadian educator)

Extracted from <www.brainyquote.com/quotes/topics/topic_friendship3.html#BtPqJbQRL8XzwWuP.9>. Accessed on October 27, 2015.

**11.** Read a story and answer the questions.

> ### Friends in the Desert
>
> Two friends were walking through the desert. During some point of the journey they had an argument, and one friend slapped the other one in the face. The one who got slapped was hurt, but without saying anything, he wrote in the sand: "Today my best friend slapped me in the face."
> They kept on walking until they found an oasis, where they decided to take a bath. The one who had been slapped got stuck in the mire and started drowning, but the friend saved him. After he recovered from the near drowning, he carved on a stone "Today my best friend saved my life."
> The friend who had slapped and saved his best friend asked him, "After I hurt you, you wrote in the sand and now, you write on a stone, why?" The other friend replied "When someone hurts us we should write it down in sand where winds of forgiveness can erase it away. But, when someone does something good for us, we must engrave it in stone where no wind can ever erase it."

VESGO, Peter; JANKI, Dadi; JOHNSON, Kelly. *Feeling Great*: Creating a Life of Optimism. Enthusiasm and Contentment. HCI, 2015. p. 46.

a. Why did the friend write on a stone, and not in the sand, "Today my best friend saved my life"?

b. What would you do if you were the friend who was saved? Would you forgive the friend who hurt you? Why?

# EXAM PRACTICE

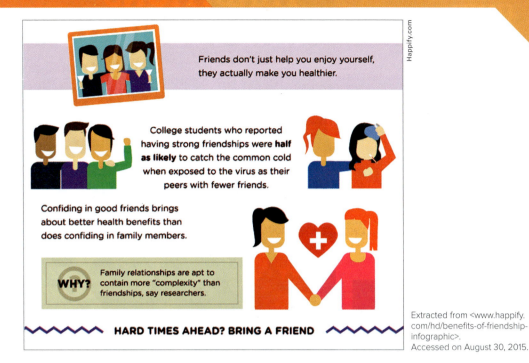

Extracted from <www.happify.com/hd/benefits-of-friendship-infographic>.
Accessed on August 30, 2015.

O texto acima é um excerto do infográfico *"Why Friends Are So Crucial to Our Happiness"*. Leia as proposições abaixo.

I. Pesquisadores da Universidade de Chicago, nos EUA, concluíram que pessoas muito solitárias tendem a ser mais indefesas, ter noites ruins de sono e sofrer mais com as complicações enfrentadas ao longo da vida, como o estresse.

Adaptado de: <www.minhavida.com.br/bem-estar/galerias/13143-oito-beneficios-que-a-amizade-traz-para-sua-vida>.
Acessado em: 2 de setembro de 2015.

II. Essa é uma necessidade natural de todo ser humano: compartilhar experiências e sensações. "A cumplicidade explica a ligação que torna os amigos inseparáveis. A compreensão que existe nesse tipo de relacionamento é profunda e marcada por muitas descobertas em conjunto, diferente do que acontece no ambiente familiar, onde as posições estão marcadas desde sempre", explica a psicóloga Marina Vasconcellos.

Extraído de: <www.minhavida.com.br/bem-estar/galerias/13143-oito-beneficios-que-a-amizade-traz-para-sua-vida/5>.
Acessado em: 2 de setembro de 2015.

III. Bons amigos são pessoas que possuem respeito, confiança, admiração, são leais e torcem pelo sucesso uns dos outros. Todas essas características são indispensáveis para criar uma equipe de trabalho unida e eficiente; por isso, é importante que as organizações incentivem a socialização entre seus profissionais.

Extraído de: <www.ibccoaching.com.br/blog/amizade-ambiente-de-trabalho-nos-torna-profissionais-mais-realizados>.
Acessado em: 2 de setembro de 2015.

Assinale a alternativa que indica as proposições claramente relacionadas ao excerto do infográfico.

**a.** Apenas II
**b.** II e III
**c.** Apenas I
**d.** I e II
**e.** I e III

# UNIT 5

# TRADITIONS AND FESTIVALS

**Nesta unidade você terá oportunidade de:**

- refletir e discutir sobre algumas tradições e festividades brasileiras;
- reconhecer os objetivos e algumas das características dos artigos de dicas de viagem e produzir um;
- compreender uma reportagem sobre uma das maiores festividades brasileiras: o bumba meu boi;
- descrever oralmente uma festividade local.

- Que festividade está representada na foto?
- Há alguma característica que indica a origem dessa festividade?
- Podemos fazer alguma conexão entre a foto e o período em que ela foi tirada?

# STARTING OUT

 Geography
History

**1.** Work in pairs. Look at the pictures and discuss what they represent. Then share your ideas with the class.

**2.** Match the passages below to the correct picture in activity 1.

- […] Probably the most well-known Brazilian New Year's Eve custom is the tradition of wearing white. […] One of the most stunning images from the night is seeing millions of people dressed in white lining the famous beach of Copacabana in Rio de Janeiro. […]

    Extracted from <newscenter.sdsu.edu/sdsu_newscenter/news_story.aspx?sid=71802>. Accessed on August 21, 2015.

- […] Capoeira is a Brazilian art form which combines fight, dance, rhythm and movement.

    Extracted from <www.princeton.edu/~capoeira/ln_abt.html>. Accessed on August 21, 2015.

- […] The state of Bahia is said to be the birthplace of Carnival in Brazil. […] In Salvador, the centre of attention is the so-called *Trio Elétrico*, creating the biggest street party in the world, according to the Guiness Book of Records.. […]

    Adapted from <www.aboutbrasil.com/modules/brazil-brasil/carnival_carnaval.php?hoofd=8&sub=46&art=494>. Accessed on August 21, 2015.

- […] This festival is held in the state of Amazonas and is the second-largest annual festival in the country (the largest being Carnival). It is held over three days during late June and celebrates a legend about an ox that was resuscitated. […]

    Extracted from <www.brazil.org.za/popular-events-in-brazil.html>. Accessed on August 21, 2015.

centre (UK)
center (US)

**3.** How can people find information about festivals, parades, and popular traditions in Brazil or around the world?

- Listening to podcasts.
- Reading magazines and newspapers headlines.
- Exploring timelines.
- Reading travel tips articles and tourism leaflets.
- Reading travel blogs.
- Others.

80  Unit 5  Traditions and Festivals

# READING COMPREHENSION

## Before Reading

**1.** Look at the banner of the online version of the newspaper *USA Today* and answer these questions aloud: Which newspaper section is the following text from? What kind of information do you expect to find in the text?

## Reading

### Cultural Traditions & Festivals in Brazil

**Danielle Hill, Demand Media**

Much of Brazil's international reputation is centered around local traditions and celebrations such as *capoeira*, the national sport and the festivities of *Carnaval*. From the cult of soccer to Catholic holidays to the rituals of the local religion, *Candomblé*, Brazil's traditions are both secular and sacred. In some cases, such as in the earthy revelry of *Carnaval*, the division seems all but clear.

Disponível em: <http://traveltips.usatoday.com/cultural-traditions-festivals-brazil-63001.html>. Acessado em: 9 de abril de 2015.

#### *Carnaval*

*Carnaval*, the traditional festival of decadence before Lent begins, has some of its biggest celebrations in Brazil. The cities of Rio de Janeiro and Salvador are particularly famous for their parades; the performers spend months preparing and practicing. During the two weeks immediately preceding the festival, local community bands play throughout Rio's neighborhoods. The informal pre-festival celebrations are known as *blocos*. Fancy balls take place throughout the city's upscale venues. The Copacabana Palace Ball is the crown jewel of these parties. In the streets, visitors watch the Samba School Parade from Sunday night through Monday morning. Major streets close to traffic throughout the *Carnaval* festivities.

#### New Year's Celebrations

Rio is home to *Réveillon*, a high-spirited New Year's celebration. Early in the day, many local restaurants serve special buffet lunches. By evening, the throngs have gathered along the city's beaches to watch the midnight fireworks display. For followers of the Afro-Brazilian religion, *Candomblé*, New Year's celebrations include wearing all-white garb, lighting candles and setting small boats loaded with trinkets into the ocean, in offering to the sea goddess *Iemanjá*.

#### *Bumba meu boi* and Regional Festivals

Throughout the year, numerous regional festivals take place in all corners of Brazil. In Sao Luís, the *Bumba meu boi* festival has the townsfolk act out a folk story involving the killing and resurrection of a bull. The celebrations span several months.

---

**TIP**

Ter bom domínio de diferentes áreas do conhecimento é muito importante, dentre outras coisas, para compreender melhor os textos. Seus conhecimentos de História e Geografia, por exemplo, podem ajudar muito na melhor compreensão de um texto sobre turismo.

---

A palavra *réveillon* é de origem francesa e deriva do verbo *réveiller*, que significa despertar. Inicialmente, esse termo era usado para designar o jantar da noite de Natal, depois passou a designar a ceia da véspera de Ano-Novo e, posteriormente, a noite da virada do ano.

Baseado em: <revistalingua.com.br/textos/blog-abizzocchi/a-origem-do-nome-reveillon-302700-1.asp>. Acessado em: 21 de novembro de 2015.

**neighbourhood** (UK)
**neighborhood** (US)

Traditions and Festivals  Unit 5  81

> In Salvador, the end of January brings a ceremonial washing of the steps of the Bonfim Church, an event that draws an audience of 800,000 people. Women in traditional costumes use perfumed water to wash the steps. Leading up to Easter, the citizens of Nova Jerusalém enact a passion play, the largest in all of South America. The stages of the cross last ten days, culminating on Easter Sunday.
>
> ### National Traditions
>
> Besides the country's animated festivals and celebrations, Brazil has numerous traditions, from sports to dance to religious rites. *Capoeira*, a home-grown martial art, is based on self-defense practices devised by African slaves. Because it was originally necessary to disguise the practice, the art now resembles dancing as much as fighting. Brazil's enthusiasm for soccer launches the sport to the level of a national obsession. Other national traditions draw from the predominant religions, Catholicism and *Candomblé*. *Candomblé* traditions include offerings to *Iemanjá* during the New Year, as well as *Boa Morte*, or beautiful death, a celebration that takes place in Salvador and incorporates music and dance. […]

Adapted from Cultural Traditions & Festivals in Brazil   Danielle Hill, Demand Media © 2011 Demand Media, Inc. U.S.A. All rights reserved.
Accessed on August 20, 2015.

**2.** Choose the best alternatives to answer the questions below.

   **a.** What is the purpose of this article?
   - To give information about festivals to tourists who want to visit Brazil.
   - To discuss the popularity of some Brazilian cultural traditions and festivals.

   **b.** What is one thing the article points out about Brazilian traditions?
   - Some Brazilian traditions combine the sacred and the profane.
   - All of them are very similar because of our past as a Portuguese colony.

**3.** Write T (True), F (False) or NM (Not Mentioned). In your notebook, copy parts from the article that correct the false statements.

   **a.** Preparation for the Carnival parades begins months before the event.

   **b.** Brazil's international reputation is completely centered on tourism.

   **c.** The sea goddess Iemanjá is revered during New Year's celebrations.

   **d.** *Capoeira* is not just a workout. It is a martial art which takes years to learn.

   **e.** *Candomblé* followers wear bright clothes during New Year's celebration.

**4.** Find the best answers to the questions.

   **a.** What do followers of *Candomblé* do to honor the sea goddess during New Year's celebrations?
   - They send small decorated boats full of candles and cheap jewelry into the ocean.
   - They wear white and gather along the beaches to honor and pray for her.

   **b.** How did African slaves disguise their *capoeira* practice?
   - They disguised it as recreational song and dance.
   - They disguised it as a dance competition.

   **c.** What can you infer about why African slaves had to disguise their *capoeira* practice?
   - Because slaves were not allowed to have any kind of entertainment even when they were not working.
   - Because it was a method of defending themselves against violent overlords.

**5.** The article presents some incorrect information about Brazilian festivities. Correct them orally and answer: why do you think that might have happened?

> "The informal pre-festival celebrations are known as *blocos*."
>
> "In the streets, visitors watch the Samba School Parade from Sunday night through Monday morning."
>
> "Rio is home to *Réveillon*, a high-spirited New Year's celebration."
>
> "[…] as well as *Boa Morte*, or beautiful death, a celebration that takes place in Salvador and incorporates music and dance. […]"

**6.** Read the following quote and answer the questions.

> "We are, at almost every point of our day, immersed in cultural diversity: faces, clothes, smells, attitudes, values, traditions, behaviours, beliefs, rituals."
> (Randa Abdel-Fattah, Australian writer)

Extracted from <www.brainyquote.com/quotes/keywords/traditions.html#gVTGrZgKJCSvhUA4.99>. Accessed on November 19, 2015.

a. Do you agree with this idea? Justify your answer.

b. In your opinion, will traditions disappear as globalization continues?

c. What could be a positive aspect of having more contact with cultural diversity around the world?

**7.** Choose the correct options to complete the sentence about some characteristics of travel tip articles.

Travel tips articles give…

a. descriptions of locations or events that might be interesting to readers.

b. background information about a city, country, or region

c. adjectives that describe the place or the event

d. a critical perspective on political issues of the place.

e. some pieces of advice from the author.

## After Reading

- Which Brazilian tradition or festival do you like the most? Why?
- Why do you think there are so many different traditions in our country? Can you give an example of one that wasn't mentioned in the text?
- Do you think that Brazilians will be celebrating the same festivities we celebrate now in 50 years?

# VOCABULARY STUDY

1. Refer back to the text on pages 81 and 82 and try to infer the meaning of the words from the box. Then use these words to complete the sentences about Carnival.

   | balls | revelry | secular | upscale | venue |
   |---|---|---|---|---|

   a. […] Brazil's Carnival festival is the most popular ♦ festival and is held in the country's streets. […]

   Adapted from <www.iberostar.com/en/hotels/brazil/pages/culture#sthash.bk3wtH3D.dpuf>. Accessed on August 21, 2015.

   b. […] Different cities in Brazil have their own way of celebrating this week-long festival of ♦ and fun. […]

   Adapted from <www.calendarlabs.com/holidays/brazil/carnival.php>. Accessed on August 21, 2015.

   c. […] Another city which is famous for its Carnival in Brazil is Salvador, Bahia. The original capital in Brazil, Carnival is celebrated a little differently here. Street Carnival is celebrated in this city rather than having a stadium as a ♦ for the parade. […]

   Adapted from <www.calendarlabs.com/holidays/brazil/carnival.php>. Accessed on August 21, 2015.

   d. […] The most elegant and ♦ of the Rio events are the Carnival balls. […]

   Extracted from <www.fest300.com/festivals/rio-carnival>. Accessed on August 21, 2015.

2. Read the following extract from the travel tips article on pages 81 and 82. Pay attention to the expression in bold and choose the correct answers to the questions.

   "Rio is home to *Réveillon*, a **high-spirited** New Year's celebration."

   a. What function does the expression in bold have?
   - It describes Rio.
   - It describes the New Year's celebration.

   b. The words in bold form a compound adjective. What is it made of?
   - An adjective + the past participle of a verb.
   - A noun + the past participle of a verb.

   > *Compound adjectives* são compostos de dois ou mais adjetivos geralmente separados por hífen quando posicionados antes do substantivo que qualificam ou descrevem.

3. Combine the words from the table to form compound adjectives and match them to the definitions below. Use each word only once.

   | Adjectives | cold | old | open | short | soft | strong |
   |---|---|---|---|---|---|---|
   | Past participles | blooded | fashioned | hearted | minded | sighted | willed |

   a. ♦ : attached to or favoring methods, ideas, or customs of an earlier time
   b. ♦ : lacking feeling or emotion
   c. ♦ : receptive to new and different ideas or the opinions of others
   d. ♦ : very sympathetic or responsive; generous in spirit
   e. ♦ : having a powerful will; resolute
   f. ♦ : relating to or suffering from myopia

   Extracted from <www.thefreedictionary.com/>. Accessed on August 21, 2015.

Unit 5   Traditions and Festivals

# LANGUAGE IN CONTEXT

## Genitive Case

1. Read three extracts from the text on pages 81 and 82 and decide whether the statements about them are T (True) or F (False).

   > "Much of **Brazil's international reputation** is centered around local traditions and celebrations such as *capoeira*, the national sport and the festivities of *Carnaval*."

   > "From the cult of soccer to Catholic holidays to the rituals of the local religion, *Candomblé*, **Brazil's traditions** are both secular and sacred. In some cases, such as in the earthy revelry of *Carnaval*, the division seems all but clear."

   > "By evening, the throngs have gatthered along the **city's beaches** to watch the midnight fireworks display."

   a. The apostrophe s ('s) used after the word Brazil is the contracted form for is.

   b. The apostrophe s ('s) used after the word Brazil shows that something belongs to or is associated with this country.

   c. The phrase in bold in the first extract could be replaced by "the international reputation of Brazil" without any change in meaning.

   d. The phrase in bold in the second extract refers to traditions which belong to Catholic holidays.

   e. The phrase in bold in the third extract refers to beaches that belong to the city.

2. Scan the travel tips article on pages 81 and 82 for other examples of the apostrophe s ('s) expressing possession or association with a noun or a noun group. Then write the phrases in your notebook.

3. Refer to activities 1 and 2 to complete the statement below.

   > In English, we often show that something belongs to or is associated with someone, something, or some place by adding ♦ to the noun and placing this possessive form ♦ the thing that is possessed by or associated with it.

   For more information about the Genitive Case, refer to Language Reference, page 175.

**4.** Read the following passages about three South African traditional events. Use the prompts in parentheses and the genitive case to complete the sentences.

**a.**

### New Year Cape style

The Kaapse Klopse, or Cape Carnival, dates back to the 19th century. It has its origins in ♦ (Cape Town / slave community), when, on a rare holiday on ♦ (New Year / Day), the ♦ (city / slaves) arranged a day of festivities. While slavery is a distant memory, this ♦ (New Year / tradition) lives on.

[…]

Cape Town's New Year celebrations

Extracted from <www.southafrica.net/za/en/articles/entry/article-southafrica.net-cape-towns-new-year>.
Accessed on November 20, 2015.

**b.**

### Two-wheel heaven

If you really want to see a country, ride a bike. ♦ (South Africa / cycling marathons) open up a world of competitiveness, exquisite scenery and fun. There are three major cycling events on every serious ♦ (cyclist / to-do list): the Cape Argus Pick n Pay Cycle Tour (every March), the Momentum 94.7 Cycle Challenge (every November), and the Absa Cape Epic (every March).

[…]

Cycling events

Extracted from <www.southafrica.net/za/en/articles/entry/article-southafrica.net-south-african-cycling-marathons>.
Accessed on November 20, 2015.

**c.**

### The toughest race of its kind in the world

The Dusi Canoe Marathon, like most river races, had its origins in ♦ (one man / love) for watercourses and his curiosity about how it ran. Ian Player helped create a legend, but every year, there are more. They say no one who has done the Dusi will ever be the same again.

[…]

The Dusi Canoe Marathon

Extracted from <www.southafrica.net/za/en/articles/entry/article-southafrica.net-the-dusi-canoe-marathon>.
Accessed on November 20, 2015.

Unit 5 Traditions and Festivals

## Possessive Adjectives

**5.** Look at the words in bold extracted from the text on pages 81 and 82. What do they refer to?

> "*Carnaval*, the traditional festival of decadence before Lent begins, has some of **its** biggest celebrations in Brazil. The cities of Rio de Janeiro and Salvador are particularly famous for **their** parades; the performers spend months preparing and practicing."

**6.** Use the words or expressions from the box to complete the text. There is one word or expression that does not suit the context.

> before   genitive case   its   object pronouns   possession   their

> Besides the ♦, another way of showing ♦ or ownership in English is using possessive adjectives. These are always positioned directly ♦ the noun they refer to. My, your, his, her, ♦, our, your, and ♦ are possessive adjectives.

**7.** The pictures below show India's biggest festival, the Kumbh Mela. Complete the captions with the correct possessive adjectives.

**coloured** (UK)
**colored** (US)

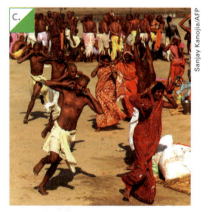

a. [...] Devotees raise ♦ hands to receive coloured holy water from a priest on the banks of the river Ganges as a rainbow shines overhead during the Kumbh Mela

b. A holy man waits for ♦ chance to take a cleansing dip during Kumbh Mela which is due to be celebrated until November

c. Bihari Hindu priests and devotees run while holding ♦ ears as part of the holy celebration

Extracted from <www.dailymail.co.uk/news/article-2291379/Kumbh-Mela-Worlds-biggest-religious-festival-comes-end-120-million-pilgrims-cleansed-sins-month-celebration.html> and <www.dailymail.co.uk/travel/travel_news/article-3232808/Leap-faith-Tens-thousands-Hindu-pilgrims-holy-dip-India-s-Kumbh-Mela-royal-bath-festival.html>. Accessed on February 24, 2016.

### WRAPPING UP

Choose one of your community's festivals and write three sentences to describe it using possessive adjectives and the genitive case. Read them to a classmate, but don't mention its name until your classmate guesses which festival you're talking about.

# LISTENING COMPREHENSION

## Before Listening

1. These are pictures of the Brazilian cities mentioned in the travel tips article on pages 81 and 82. Do you know which landmarks they show? Where are they located?

2. Identify the names of the cities in the pictures according to the celebrations they are famous for.

   a. New Year's Celebration: ♦

   b. Washing of the steps of the *Nosso Senhor do Bonfim* Church: ♦

   c. *Bumba meu boi* festival: ♦

88 Unit 5 Traditions and Festivals

## Listening

 **3.** A reporter from the BBC visits the city of São Luís during the *bumba meu boi* festival and talks to Nadir, a local citizen, who tells him that it's the most important day to the people of Maranhão. Listen and answer: Why is it important?

> Observe que o jornalista, ao falar sobre a festividade, usa o tempo presente dos verbos, bem como diferentes adjetivos.

 **4.** Complete the sentences with the words from the box. Then listen to the recording again and check your answers.

> embroidered    fantastic    inventive    nervous    poor

a. The Florestans feel ♦ as time approaches for their moment in the public spotlight.

b. In the news reporter's opinion, their performance was ♦.

c. They were wearing richly ♦ costumes and original ♦ masks.

d. The people of Floresta live in a ♦ part of the city.

## After Listening

What do you think the news reporter means when he says, "They shine the brightest"? Justify your views.

# SPEAKING

✓ In pairs, think of different festivals that take place in your city or region.

✓ Decide on which of them is the most important. Talk about the reasons why it is the most important festival, when it happens and what the community does to celebrate it.

✓ Present your ideas to the whole group. Use the phrases from the box to help you.

> ▶ **USEFUL LANGUAGE**
>
> One of (name of your city)'s biggest/most important/most famous festival is…
>
> The festival is celebrated on…
>
> We celebrate…
>
> People from the city…
>
> That is a very important day for us because…
>
> The festival takes place in…
>
> The celebration includes…

# WRITING

In pairs, write a travel tips article about a festivity or celebration that takes place in a Brazilian city or region.

## Planning your travel tips article

- Talk to your classmate and decide which festivity or celebration both of you would like to write about.
- Do some research about it on the Internet.
- Don't forget to look for information about cultural, historical, and social aspects of the festivity or celebration you have chosen.
- If possible, look for some images to illustrate your travel tips article.

## Writing and rewriting your article

- Write a draft of the article in your notebook.

> **REFLECTING AND EVALUATING**
>
> Go back to your travel tips article and make sure you paid attention to the following topics:
> - ✓ Are the descriptions attractive to readers?
> - ✓ Is there enough information about the festivity or celebration?
> - ✓ Does it present a closing paragraph inviting people to the event?
> - ✓ Have you checked grammar, punctuation, and spelling?

- Show your draft to your teacher and ask him/her to correct it.
- After the correction, make all the necessary adjustments and write a clean copy of the article.

## After writing

- If possible, publish your article on the school website, or post it on a blog so you can share your findings about the festivity or celebration you have chosen and help others to decide on their next travel destination.
- Alternatively, gather all the articles and make a book of Brazilian festivities and celebrations.
- Donate the book to the school library and invite students to read it.

# SELF-ASSESSMENT

Chegamos ao fim da unidade 5. Convidamos você a refletir sobre seu desempenho até aqui e responder às questões propostas abaixo, escolhendo uma das seguintes opções:

Sim.          Preciso me preparar mais.

### Questões

- Você é capaz de identificar diferentes tipos de festividades brasileiras, reconhecer nelas algumas características típicas da região de origem e discutir sobre a importância dessas tradições para a cultura do país?
- Você se considera apto a ler e compreender artigos de dicas de viagem e reconhecer as características principais inerentes ao gênero?
- Você reúne conhecimentos linguístico-discursivos suficientes para produzir um artigo de dicas de viagem em inglês?
- Você se considera preparado para escutar reportagens sobre festividades brasileiras, compreender os motivos para tais comemorações, bem como identificar os adjetivos que as caracterizam?
- Você se julga apto a discutir sobre uma festividade de relevância em sua região?

### Refletindo sobre suas respostas

- De que forma suas práticas de aprendizagem no decorrer desta unidade influenciaram suas respostas?
- O que você pode fazer para aprimorar ainda mais os conhecimentos adquiridos nesta unidade?
    a. Procurar conhecer mais sobre as festividades que ocorrem em diferentes regiões do país, sua origem e a forma como são celebradas.
    b. Ler mais artigos de dicas de viagem, ampliando meus conhecimentos sobre diferentes regiões do país, bem como sobre as festividades típicas de cada uma delas.
    c. Aprofundar meus conhecimentos em língua inglesa, usando recursos diversos, de forma que minha participação nas atividades seja mais ativa.
    d. Outros.

# UNIT 6

# MY TWO MOMS

**Nesta unidade você terá oportunidade de:**

- refletir e posicionar-se criticamente sobre as famílias formadas por pessoas de mesmo sexo;
- reconhecer os objetivos e algumas das características dos relatos pessoais e produzir um;
- compreender o trecho de um filme no qual uma adolescente relata sua experiência sobre ter sido criada por dois pais;
- compartilhar com a turma seu ponto de vista sobre a liberação do casamento entre pessoas do mesmo sexo em alguns países.

- O que a imagem representa?
- Ela mostra uma ação comum à época atual?
- Em quais sociedades o casamento retratado na foto pode ter acontecido?

# STARTING OUT

 Biology
Sociology

1. The artworks below, created for the IDAHOT 2015, became widespread memes. In pairs, discuss: what message do they convey?

> A palavra "meme" designa uma ideia ou um conceito que se difunde rapidamente pela internet. Uma frase, um vídeo, uma imagem ou uma música podem, assim, se transformar em um meme.
>
> Baseado em: <www.infoescola.com/comunicacao/memes/>. Acessado em: 10 de setembro de 2015.

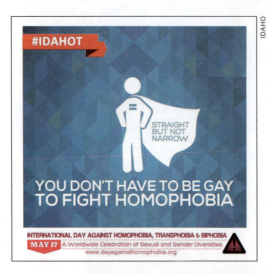

Extracted from <dayagainsthomophobia.org/idahot-memes/#prettyPhoto>. Accessed on August 24, 2015.

> O Dia Internacional Contra a Homofobia, Lesbofobia e Transfobia (IDAHOT — *The International Day Against Homophobia, Transphobia and Biphobia*) comemora-se a 17 de maio, data em que, em 1990, a Organização Mundial da Saúde retirou a homossexualidade de sua Classificação Internacional de Doenças.
>
> Baseado em: <diversidade.pr5.ufrj.br/index.php/2-uncategorised/64-17-de-maio-dia-internacional-de-combate-a-homofobia-lesbofobia-e-transfobia>. Acessado: em 21 de novembro de 2015.

2. Read these quotes and choose the one that best relates to the ideas conveyed by the memes in activity 1.

   a. "What is straight? A line can be straight, or a street, but the human heart, oh, no, it's curved like a road through mountains." (Tennessee Williams, American playwright)
   Extracted from <www.goodreads.com/quotes/438902-what-is-straight-a-line-can-be-straight-or-a>. Accessed on November 21, 2015.

   b. "Friendship… is born at that moment when one man says to another: 'What! You too? I thought that no one but myself …'" (C.S. Lewis, Irish writer)
   Extracted from <www.goodreads.com/quotes/tag/friendship>. Accessed on August 24, 2015.

   c. "It seems to me that we generally do not have a correct measure of our own wisdom." (R.K. Narayan, Indian author)
   Extracted from <www.goodreads.com/quotes/work/quotes/125088-the-guide>. Accessed on November 21, 2015.

3. Why do some people who have experienced discrimination or violence decide to write personal narratives about what happened to them? Would you write one? Why/Why not? Talk to a classmate and then share your opinions with the whole class.

Unit 6 My Two Moms

# READING COMPREHENSION

## Before Reading

1. Look at the picture below and answer the question: what kind of relationship do these people seem to have?

## Reading

**realise** (UK) **realize** (US)
**mum** (UK) **mom** (US)

### Lesbian mothers: My two mums

*A recent study found that children raised by lesbian couples were often brighter, happier and more confident than kids brought up in more traditional family units.*

[...]

**ASHLING PHILLIPS AND NATALIE DREW**

*Ashling, 32, and Natalie, 35, have been together for nine years and live in Birmingham. They have two children, Giana, five, and Kai, two*

**NATALIE:** My family didn't take my coming out very well. They were so homophobic that I moved out at 17. It was only after Ashling and I got together that there was some level of acceptance. Having our children has brought the whole family closer together. They've accepted us and realise that times have changed.

**ASHLING:** Natalie and I had been friends for 17 years. We both went off to university, and when I moved back to Birmingham nine years ago, we got together.

**NATALIE:** I'd always wanted kids and a few of my gay male friends had offered to donate sperm. We thought it would cause complications, so we researched agencies online and found they were charging huge amounts. We didn't trust the process. How do you know it's what you ordered?

**ASHLING:** We decided to find a private donor and do it ourselves. We found Ben on a sperm-donor website and arranged to meet. We got along well, and after we'd all had a health check, he fathered our two kids. He's in their lives and sees them two or three times a year. They know him as Daddy Ben, and we've tried to keep everything as open and honest as possible.

**NATALIE:** You'd be surprised how many men want to help women in our situation. After our experience, we decided to set up gayfamilyweb.co.uk, offering to connect gay families with donors and other gay families. It was difficult for us to meet other gay women with children in our area – although we had the support of our straight friends, we felt isolated as we had no one to talk to in the same situation.

**ASHLING:** It's been difficult at times because I think people in our town weren't exposed to gay families before. Overall we've been accepted by our community, but every now and then there's a little reminder that people don't know how to deal with gay families. The week before Father's Day this year, Giana's class made cards, and because her school wasn't sure what to do with her, they got her to make a card for her little brother instead. She's young and didn't understand why she was asked to make a card for her brother while all the other children made cards for their dads. The school knows that Natalie and I are together – they just didn't know how to deal with the dad issue. […]

Extracted from <www.theguardian.com/lifeandstyle/2010/dec/12/lesbian-mothers-my-two-mums>. Accessed on August 23, 2015.

**2.** Choose the best option to complete the sentence below.

Natalie and Ashling's personal narratives are mainly about…

  **a.** all the difficulties they overcame to conceive their own children.

  **b.** sharing their experiences as mothers with other gay families.

  **c.** their struggle to get together and build a family.

**3.** Complete the sentences. Write *Ashling*, *Ben*, *Natalie*, or *Natalie's gay male friends*.

  **a.** ♦ offered to help the couple.

  **b.** ♦ got along well with the couple and became the sperm donor.

  **c.** ♦ says that the donor is involved in their children's lives.

  **d.** ♦ left home because her family was homophobic and couldn't accept her homosexuality.

**4.** Identify the only statement you can infer about Natalie and Ashling.

  **a.** Natalie and Ashling have never had enough courage to confront their families.

  **b.** The couple's kids do not understand the kind of family they belong to.

  **c.** The relationship between the kids and their "Daddy Ben" is not good because Ben lives in another country.

  **d.** Life isn't that easy for Natalie and Ashling, but, despite everything, they're happy and live a very open and honest life with their kids.

  **e.** In Birmingham, people don't seem to have had much exposure to gay families.

> **TIP**
> Lembre-se de acionar seus conhecimentos prévios e de mundo para fazer inferências. Levante hipóteses, reflita e estabeleça conexões com o texto que você leu.

**5.** Write an explanation to the sentence you checked in activity 4. If necessary, use a dictionary to help you.

**6.** Answer the questions below in your notebook.

  **a.** Why did Natalie and Ashling refuse a sperm donation from their gay male friends? How do you interpret this?

  **b.** Why do you think Natalie and Ashling decided to speak up about their lives as lesbian moms in a widely read newspaper like *The Guardian*? Would you do the same? Justify your answer.

**7.** Read another extract from Ashling's personal narrative. Then discuss the questions that follow with a classmate.

> **ASHLING:** The one issue people tend to bring up is the concept of the absent father figure and the effect that will have on the children, especially Kai. We've made a conscious decision to ensure there are strong male role models around.

Extracted from <www.theguardian.com/lifeandstyle/2010/dec/12/lesbian-mothers-my-two-mums>. Accessed on March 24, 2016.

In your opinion, why do people show concern about the effects of the absent father on the children? Do you agree with them?

**8.** Match the parts to form sentences about the characteristics of personal narratives.

  **a.** Personal narratives tell

  **b.** The text is centered on the narrator, so

  **c.** The author expresses his/her opinions, feelings, impressions,

  **d.** There are usually

  **e.** Personal narratives include specific details about

  **1.** the pronouns *I*, *me*, and the possessive adjective *my* are very commonly used.

  **2.** adjectives in personal narratives.

  **3.** the time, place, and people involved.

  **4.** a fact or an experience that the author has been through.

  **5.** and points of view about the facts.

## After Reading

- In your opinion, what do families need to do to raise children properly?
- Do you think that both traditional families and homosexual couples can do it? Explain.
- How would people in your community deal with a family like Natalie and Ashling's? Justify your answer.

# VOCABULARY STUDY

1. Go back to the personal narrative on pages 95 and 96 and find the words or expressions that match the meanings below.

    a. ♦ : make more or less public acknowledgment of being homosexual.

    b. ♦ : a person or animal providing blood, an organ, bone marrow cells, or other biological tissue for transfusion or transplantation.

    c. ♦ : any problem or difficulty.

    d. ♦ : to grasp or understand clearly.

    e. ♦ : (informal) a heterosexual.

    Extracted from <dictionary.reference.com>. Accessed on November 21, 2015.

2. Now read what another couple, Seema and Daksha, said about the benefits and the challenges of bringing up children with two moms. Then use the words from activity 1 to complete the text. Make all the necessary adjustments.

    a. […] SEEMA: I grew up in a Muslim Asian family in Blackburn. I ♦ to my siblings when I was 16 and they were fine with it, but I didn't come out to my parents for a long time. […]

    b. […] SEEMA: We decided we were going to have our civil partnership in 2006. My mother adores Daksha, so she was pleased initially, but when she ♦ we were having a registration ceremony and a big Asian wedding, like a ♦ couple would, she was anxious about what people would say. […]

    c. […] DAKSHA: I always wanted a child. We asked friends to ask their friends if they'd be a ♦, and when one said yes it turned out we knew him already. It was important to us that he was Asian, as we figured Lia would have enough to contend with without having to deal with ♦ about her nationality, too. […]

    Extracted from <www.theguardian.com/lifeandstyle/2010/dec/12/lesbian-mothers-my-two-mums>. Accessed on August 24, 2015.

3. In the word *homophobic*, extracted from "They were so **homophobic** that I moved out at 17", what does the suffix *-phobic* mean? Choose the correct alternative.

    a. the same, identical; relating to the same family.

    b. suffering from fear or antipathy; relating to a phobia.

4. Look up for the meanings of the words below in an English-English dictionary then compose and complete the table below in your notebook.

| Phobia | Meaning |
| --- | --- |
| acrophobia | ♦ |
| agoraphobia | ♦ |
| anthropophobia | ♦ |
| glossophobia | ♦ |
| xenophobia | ♦ |

98  Unit 6  My Two Moms

# LANGUAGE IN CONTEXT

## Present Perfect II

1. Read the following extracts from the personal narrative on pages 95 and 96 and find the verbs that indicate actions which started in the past and continue up to the present or that have consequences in the present. Then pick out the correct answers to the questions below.

   > "Having our children has brought the whole family closer together."
   > "Ashling, 32, and Natalie, 35, have been together **for** nine years and live in Birmingham."

   a. **Has** the fact of having children **affected** Natalie's family?

      1. No, it hasn't. Her family hasn't been affected at all.

      2. Yes, it has. It has made her family closer.

   b. How long **have** Ashling and Natalie **been** together?

      1. They have been together **since** they were 23 and 26 years of age, respectively.

      2. They have been together **since** their children were nine years old.

2. Pay attention to the structures in bold in the previous activity. Then complete the sentences accordingly.

   a. The verb forms *has affected* and *have been* refer to situations that happened in the past and have consequences in the ♦ or continue up to the present.

   b. We use ♦ before the period of duration of an action and ♦ before the beginning of that period.

   c. In interrogative sentences in the Present Perfect tense, we use ♦ or *has* before the subject and the past participle of the main verb after the subject.

   d. *Yes + subject + have /* ♦ are positive short answers and *No + subject + haven't /* ♦ are negative short answers.

   For more information about the Present Perfect, go to Language Reference, pages 176 and 177.

3. Based on the text on pages 95 and 96, write short answers to the questions below in your notebook. Then complete your answers with information from the text.

   a. Has Ben seen Giana and Kai lately?

   b. Have Ashling and Natalie had difficulties meeting other gay women with children?

**4.** Use *for* or *since* to complete the extracts below. Then use the prompts to write complete statements in the Present Perfect tense.

"It's complex, but what families aren't complicated?": Daksha, Seema and baby Lia.

**a.** […] Daksha, 39, and Seema, 45, have been together ♦ 10 years. They had a traditional Indian civil wedding in 2006 and have a 15-month-old daughter, Lia. […]

<sub>Extracted from <www.theguardian.com/lifeandstyle/2010/dec/12/lesbian-mothers-my-two>. Accessed on August 24, 2015.</sub>

Daksha and Seema / be married / 2006

**b.** […] DAKSHA: "I've been out to my family ♦ I was 17." […]

<sub>Extracted from <www.theguardian.com/lifeandstyle/2010/dec/12/lesbian-mothers-my-two-mums>. Accessed on August 24, 2015.</sub>

Daksha / be out to her family / a long time

## Comparatives

**5.** Read the extract below and pay attention to the structures in bold. Then answer the questions in your notebook.

> "A recent study found that children raised by lesbian couples were often **brighter, happier** and **more confident than** kids brought up in more traditional family units."

**a.** Who does the writer compare children raised by lesbian couples to?

**b.** Do children raised by lesbian couples show the same degree of intelligence, happiness and self-confidence as those raised in traditional families?

**c.** In the extract above, which words are used to compare children brought up in different circumstances?

**6.** Match the columns to form meaningful statements about the comparatives in English.

> **Irregular Comparatives**
> **good** – better
> **bad** – worse
> **far** – farther / further

a. To form the comparatives of superiority of most short adjectives like bright and happy, for example,

b. To form the comparatives of superiority of most long adjectives like confident, for example,

c. The second element of the comparison is

- we use *more* before those adjectives.

- we add *-er* to those adjectives.

- preceded by the word *than*.

For spelling rules when forming the comparative, go to Language Reference, page 178.

**7.** Use the comparative form of the adjectives from the box to complete the text below.

> good    harmonious    healthy    high    small

### Major New Study Finds Kids Raised By Same-Sex Couples Are '♦ And Happier'

BY JUDD LEGUM, JUL 5, 2014 8:19PM

It's the rallying cry for opponents of same-sex marriage: "Every child deserves a mom or a dad." But a major new study finds that kids raised by same-sex couples actually do a bit ♦ " ♦ the general population on measures of general health and family cohesion."

The study, conducted in Australia by University of Melbourne researchers "surveyed 315 same-sex parents and 500 children." The children in the study scored about six percent ♦ Australian kids in the general population. The advantages held up "when controlling for a number of sociodemographic factors such as parent education and household income." The study was the largest of its kind in the world.

The lead researcher, Dr. Simon Crouch, noted that in same-sex couples, parents have to "take on roles that are suited to their skill sets rather than falling into those gender stereotypes." According to Crouch, this leads to a "♦ family unit and therefore feeding on to better health and well-being."

The findings were in line with "existing international research undertaken with ♦ sample sizes." […]

Adapted from <thinkprogress.org/lgbt/2014/07/05/3456717/kids-raised-by-same-sex-couples-are-healthier-and-happier/>. Accessed on November 27, 2015.

### WRAPPING UP

In pairs, answer the questions: What have you done to make your voice heard and support gender equality? How have you worked for a non-sexist society? Remember to use the Present Perfect tense in your answers. Then report them to the class.

# LISTENING COMPREHENSION

## Before Listening

1. The infographic below shows the countries with national laws allowing same-sex marriage. In pairs, look at the infographic attentively and answer the following questions:
   - Where and when did gay marriage first become legal?
   - Where did it become legal in 2015?
   - Did most of the countries legalize gay marriage soon after the Netherlands did, or have most legalized it only in the past few years?
   - Which South American countries recognize gay marriage?

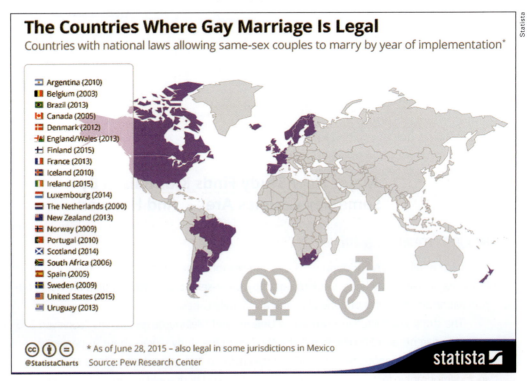

Extracted from <www.statista.com/chart/3594/the-countries-where-gay-marriage-is-legal/>. Accessed on August 25, 2015.

## Listening

2. You are going to listen to a young girl, who is a child of LGBT parents, talk about her experience and her views on what it means to be a family. Read the sentences below and write T (True) or F (False).

   a. She was put up for adoption because her birth mother wasn't able to take care of her.

   b. Her birth mother didn't like her parents' letter too much, but met them because they were the only couple who wanted to adopt a child at that time.

   c. The young girl says she has ups and downs with her family, and that's why she doesn't feel comfortable talking to them about some issues.

   d. She does a lot of family things with her parents.

**3.** In your notebook, rewrite the false sentences from activity 2 with the correct information.

**4.** Listen to the second part of the recording and complete the sentences with the missing information. Use your own words:

a. The young girl says some friends are cool to her family, but they say ♦

b. In her opinion, people who don't have LGBT parents should be aware of the things they say because ♦

c. She says everyone ♦

## After Listening

Read and discuss the extract below with a classmate. Do you agree with the young girl's point of view? Justify.

> "And you know, we're no different. We're all the same, you know, in the sense that we all just wanna be kinda cared for. We all wanna be loved. And uhm, just kind of be aware of your surroundings and try to make them more comforta...a more comfortable place and a safer place for everyone."

### PRONUNCIATION PRACTICE

The words below are spoken by two native speakers, an American and an English man. Listen and pay attention to the way they pronounce the "r" sound.

    mother    letter    lawyer

Now listen to the pronunciation of the following words and look for the ones that are pronounced the British way.

    better    later    power    remember    other

# SPEAKING

In small groups, discuss the questions below. Use expressions from the Useful Language where appropriate.

✓ Should all the countries in the world allow same-sex marriage? Why/Why not?

✓ How differently do people live in countries where same-sex marriage has been allowed? Do you think they are happier somehow? Explain.

✓ Has anything changed in Brazil since 2013, when same-sex marriage became legal? What exactly?

### ▶ USEFUL LANGUAGE

| | |
|---|---|
| I agree up to a point, but… | I'm not so sure about that. |
| I agree with you in part, but… | It is not as simple as it seems. |
| I see your point, but… | That's true, but… |

# WRITING

Write your own personal narrative. Follow the steps below.

## Planning your personal narrative

- Think of an issue that you would like to write about on a personal level. Here are some suggestions:

    It can be …
    - something that made you happy, sad, or even worried.
    - related to friends, family, prejudice, social injustice, relationships, school routine, or a community problem that affects you.
    - a change in your life or a realization.

- Set up the tone of your narrative.
- Take notes of facts, your feelings, and opinions.

## Writing and rewriting your text

- Write a draft of your personal narrative in your notebook.

### REFLECTING AND EVALUATING

Go back to your personal narrative and make sure you paid attention to the following topics:

✓ Did you report your personal experience with a beginning, a middle, and an end?
✓ Did you make clear the effects of that experience had on you?
✓ Is your personal narrative written in the first person singular?
✓ Did you use words that are appropriate to the maturity of your audience?
✓ Is it written in the past tense?
✓ Did you check the punctuation and paragraphs?

- Ask a classmate to read and make comments on your personal narrative.
- Write a clean copy making all the necessary adjustments.

## After writing

- If possible, publish your personal narrative on the school website.
- Alternatively, you and your classmates can produce a mural called "Don't let in, spill it out" and share personal experiences.

# SELF-ASSESSMENT

Chegamos ao fim da unidade 6. Convidamos você a refletir sobre seu desempenho até aqui e responder às questões propostas abaixo, escolhendo uma das seguintes opções:

Sim.    Preciso me preparar mais.

### Questões

- Você adquiriu repertório suficiente para discutir e posicionar-se criticamente sobre as famílias formadas por pessoas do mesmo sexo?
- Você se considera apto a ler e compreender um relato pessoal em língua inglesa e reconhecer as características principais inerentes ao gênero?
- Você reúne conhecimentos linguístico-discursivos suficientes para produzir um relato pessoal em língua inglesa?
- Você se sente preparado para escutar trechos de filmes nos quais alguns adolescentes relatam sua experiência de terem sido criados por famílias constituídas por pessoas do mesmo sexo e compreender os sentimentos por eles expressos?
- Você se julga apto a expor seu ponto de vista sobre a liberação do casamento entre as pessoas do mesmo sexo em algumas sociedades, bem como contra argumentar, se necessário?

### Refletindo sobre suas respostas

- Como você analisa a evolução do seu aprendizado em relação à unidade anterior?
- De que forma suas práticas de aprendizagem no decorrer desta unidade influenciaram suas respostas?
- O que você pode fazer para aprimorar ainda mais os conhecimentos adquiridos nesta unidade?
    a. Buscar por mais informações sobre a liberação do casamento entre pessoas do mesmo sexo em diferentes sociedades, de que forma essa conquista se deu e qual a repercussão disso nos locais em questão.
    b. Ler mais depoimentos para desenvolver melhor minha capacidade de compreensão e análise crítica.
    c. Aprofundar meus conhecimentos em língua inglesa, usando recursos diversos, de forma que minha participação nas atividades seja mais ativa.
    d. Outros.

# Further Practice 3 – Units 5 & 6

**1.** Look at the cover of the travel guide below and decide who, besides tourists, would be interested in reading it.

### Inti Raymi: the Festival of the Sun

Every year in June, there is an opportunity to witness a beautiful exhibition of Peruvian culture and tradition: *Inti Raymi*, the Festival of the Sun.

The *Inti Raymi* festival originated as a celebration to honor the Sun God as insurance for plentiful crops in the harvest season. Each winter solstice, when the sun is farthest from the earth, the Inca would gather out of fear of the lack of the sun, beseeching its return. In 1572, the colonial Spaniards banned the tradition because of its pagan rituals.

The festivities went underground, but today it is celebrated as one of the largest festivals in South America, second only to the Carnival of Rio. Every year, hundreds of thousands of people gather in Cusco for the week-long-festivities. From live music to street vendors to daytime fairs, the festival consists of different daily activities. Free concerts, put on by the best Peruvian musical troupes, are held nightly in the Plaza de Armas.

All activities lead up to June 24, the climax of the festival and the actual day of *Inti Raymi*. Scientifically speaking the winter solstice begins June 21, but Peruvians follow the pacha unachaq, a sundial used by the Inca.
Over 500 actors are selected to enact the day-long ceremony. It is considered a great honor to be selected as Sapa Inca or his wife, as they are the two main characters for the day. Ceremonies commence in the Qorikancha square in front of the Santo Domingo Church, which is built over the Temple of the Sun. Here Sapa Inca calls blessings from the sun. Afterwards, he is carried on a golden throne to Sacsayhuamán, a fortress in the hills above Cusco. Thousands of people await his arrival. He climbs the sacred altar. A White Llama is sacrificed to ensure the fertility of the earth.

At sunset, haystacks are set afire and revelers dance around them to honor the Empire of the Four Wind Directions. The ceremony ends with the celebrants returning to Cusco, watching as Sapa Inca and Mama Occla are carried on their golden thrones. And so the sun's new year begins!

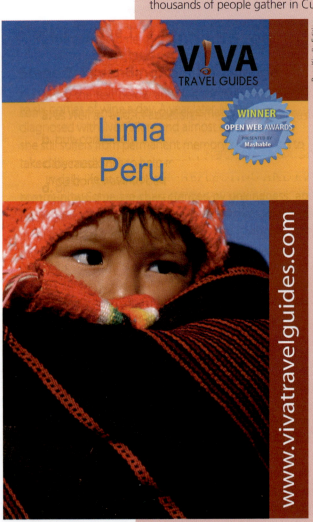

SEGREDA, Rick; NEWTON Paula; CAPUTO Lorraine. *VIVA Travel Guides Peru*. Viva Publishing Network, 2010. p. 27

**2.** Choose the correct alternatives to complete the sentences.

a. The festival celebrates
   1. plentiful crops.
   2. the Sun God.

b. The festival takes place in
   1. the city of Cusco.
   2. different places in Peru, simultaneously.

c. The Festival of the Sun was banned in 1572 because
   1. white Llamas were sacrificed.
   2. the celebration was contrary to the Catholic faith.

**3.** Match the expressions from the circle to the correct information about them.

1. Carnival in Rio de Janeiro
2. Duration of *Inti Raymi*
3. The day of the festival
4. The location of the festivities
5. A great honor for actors

a. To play Sapa Inca or his wife, Mama Occla
b. June 24
c. The largest festival in South America
d. All week long
e. Plaza de Armas

**4.** Read the travel guide excerpt again. Find the passage which corresponds to the pictures below. Then copy it in your notebook.

Inti Raymi, the Festival of the Sun, is the annual recreation of an important Inca ceremony in the city of Cuzco, Peru, South America. Photo of June 24, 2013.

Units 5 & 6  **Further Practice 3**  107

# Further Practice 3 – Units 5 & 6

**5.** The characters in the comic strip below are the seagull Ollie and the lugworm Quentin. Read the comic strip and identify the only false sentence.

**a.** Ollie isn't sure about what La Tomatina is.

**b.** Quentin knows more about La Tomatina than Ollie.

**c.** Only Quentin thinks that a tradition like La Tomatina should be started in Bigley Bay.

**d.** Ollie probably changed his mind about starting a similar tradition in Bigley Bay.

**6.** Read the text below. Then write T (True), F (False) or NM (Not Mentioned).

BUNOL, Spain – August 26: Revellers enjoy the atmosphere in tomato pulp while participating the annual Tomatina festival on August 26, 2015 in Bunol, Spain. An estimated 22,000 people threw 150 tons of ripe tomatoes in the world's biggest tomato fight held annually in this Spanish Mediterranean town.

David Ramos/Getty Images

### Top 5 Spanish Celebrations

3rd September 2014
by Steven Douglas

If there's one thing Spain knows how to do, Spain definitely knows how to put on a celebration! Throughout the year, all throughout Spain, different provinces and cities host different types of celebrations that are elaborate, colorful, as well as exciting! If you're ever in Spain during these times, we highly suggest you go and experience these celebrations because they are events that you will never forget! Here are some of Spain's biggest and best celebrations!

[...]

#### 4. LA TOMATINA

Where: Buñol

When: August

Sure you love tomatoes on your salad or sandwiches but what about… a tomato fight? Things are definitely going to get really messy with this celebration as people gather in one spot and have a full-on tomato fight, creating a war field of flying tomatoes.

By the end of it, you'll be a red, drippy mess and people enjoy it because they keep celebrating every single year! Don't worry — there are communal showers set up so that you can cleanse yourself off once the battle is over. Definitely not for everyone, but you know what they say, when in Spain, do as the locals do!

[...]

Adapted from <blog.trip4real.com/top-5-spanish-celebrations/>. Accessed on November 23, 2015.

a. Celebrations in Spain take place during one specific period of the year and in one or two cities.

b. Food fights like La Tomatina are criticized by organizations that fight world hunger.

c. According to the text, celebrations in Spain are memorable.

d. Neighbors offer their showers to the participants of La Tomatina so they can clean themselves up once the celebration is over.

e. There are tomato fights all over the town of Buñol.

**7.** Match the parts of the text that correct the false statements in the previous activity.

1. "[…] there are communal showers set up so that you can cleanse yourself off once the battle is over."

2. "Throughout the year, all throughout Spain, different provinces and cities host different types of celebrations that are elaborate, colorful, as well as exciting!"

3. "[…] people gather in one spot and have a full-on tomato fight, creating a war field of flying tomatoes."

**8.** Read the quote and answer the question.

When I was a child I asked my mother what homosexuality was about and she said – and this was 100 years ago in Germany and she was very open-minded – "It's like hair color. It's nothing. Some people are blond and some people have dark hair. It's not a subject." This was a very healthy attitude.

(Karl Lagerfeld, German fashion designer)

Extracted from <www.brainyquote.com/quotes/quotes/k/karllager472624.html>.
Accessed on September 5, 2015.

- What did Karl's mother's mean when she compared homosexuality to hair color?

# Further Practice 3 – Units 5 & 6

**9.** Read Aspen's personal narrative and choose the best alternative to complete it.

> **Son tells of life with pioneer gay couple: "It's so cool how I was born. Dad and Daddy both really wanted me".**
>
> By ASPEN DREWITT-BARLOW, 11, whose dads Barrie and Tony were the first gay couple in Britain to have a baby through a surrogate mother.
>
> *As well as Aspen and his twin Saffron, the family from Danbury, Essex, have been joined by Orlando, now seven, and 10-month-old twins Dallas and Jasper.*
>
> People might think my life is very different from other children who have a mum and a dad but it's not. It's just like any other 11-year-old's, except there's not a mum and a dad, there are two dads.
>
> I always get asked that. "What's the difference between having two dads, and a mum and dad?"
>
> I wouldn't know because it ♦ this way. I've got two dads and we've got two mums as well – our surrogate mum and the one whose eggs we came from.
>
> I first ♦ our family was a bit different when I was about eight or nine and other kids started asking questions like, "Where's your mum?" and "Why have you got two dads?".
>
> Now I'm used to being asked, so I just tell them the truth. There are people who think it's fine to be gay but it bothers some others. That's what it comes down to a lot of the time.
>
> Tony is Dad, Barrie is Daddy.
>
> [...]
>
> Once, a boy ♦ that I'll follow in my dads' footsteps. He meant by being gay but I told him: "Yeah, I'll be rich and famous." He didn't say anything after that.
>
> It does hurt to hear people say things but I ♦ other children called names for other reasons. At the same school some children got picked on for having dark skin, which wasn't fair either.
>
> I'm at another school now and it's much better. And I think things have got better for families with two dads or two mums in general. [...]

Jul 03, 2006; Chelmsford, Essex, UK; Britain's first gay dads share big day with children, surrogate mothers and egg donor. Gay dads Barrie Drewitt-Barlow and Tony Drewitt Barlow today tied the knot at a civil partnership ceremony before friends and family at Hylands House at Chelmsford in Essex. They are pictured with their three children.

Extracted from <www.mirror.co.uk/news/uk-news/son-tells-of-life-with-pioneer-gay-272119>. Accessed on November 27, 2015.

a. 's always been – realised – said – 've heard

b. 's always – realised – has said – heard

c. was – have realised – said – 've heard

**10.** Answer the questions below. Then share your view with the class.

a. What do you think about Aspen's personal narrative? What can you infer about him?

b. If you were Aspen, how would you deal with people's questions and opinions?

# EXAM PRACTICE

## May 17 – The International Day Against Homophobia

The International Day Against Homophobia (or IDAHO, as it is sometimes known) is celebrated around the world on May 17. This annual day to mark the fight to make our society inclusive of all sexualities was founded in Montreal in 2003 by the human rights group Fondation Émergence. It was quickly embraced across Canada, and then internationally.

But the public acceptance of a day of action is certainly not the same thing as an acceptance of the equality of the LGBT communities (self-identifying Lesbian, Gay, Bisexual, and Transgendered persons). Around the world, people who identify themselves as LGBT are still ostracized, the victims of hate crimes, and the targets of systemic repression. This is unacceptable, and we join in the cause of making homophobia a thing of the past.

What makes this a union issue? Like all human rights issues, the struggle to end homophobia is part of the overall struggle for the simple respect and dignity to which every human being should be entitled.

[...]

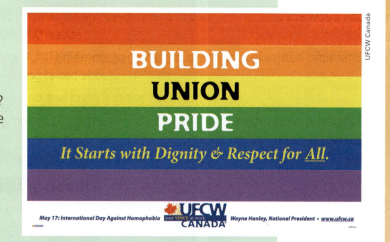

Adaptado de: <www.ufcw.ca/index.php?option=com_content&view=article&id=1056:may-17-the-international-day-against-homophobia&catid=24&Itemid=5&lang=en>. Acessado em: 6 de setembro de 2015.

Em última instância, o texto nos leva a concluir que...

a. a homossexualidade não é um desvio de conduta e muito menos uma condição patológica; portanto, a homofobia não se justifica e é um crime que deve ser combatido em todo o mundo.

b. a sociedade pode ser considerada corresponsável por crimes cometidos contra a população LGBT, uma vez que não se posiciona claramente contra essa realidade.

c. cada indivíduo precisa ser respeitado em sua individualidade e, assim, ter assegurada sua dignidade.

d. A população LGBT deve abandonar o ostracismo social e abarcar a luta da qual certamente sairá beneficiada e fortalecida em seus direitos.

e. Os governantes precisam investir mais em educação para a aceitação e a tolerância das minorias sociais, visando à superação da homofobia no mundo.

# UNIT 7

# ALCOHOL CONSUMPTION

PhuShutter/Shutterstock.com

**Nesta unidade você terá oportunidade de:**

- refletir e se posicionar criticamente sobre o consumo de bebidas alcoólicas e os prejuízos que elas causam em nosso organismo;

- reconhecer os objetivos e algumas das características dos relatórios de pesquisas, bem como produzir um;

- compreender um anúncio sobre dependência de bebidas alcoólicas;

- analisar e discutir dados em um mapa.

- Qual a relação entre a imagem e o título da unidade?
- Você já viu algum símbolo parecido com este em algum lugar? O que esse símbolo significa?

SAY NO!

# STARTING OUT

Biology
Sociology

**1.** How much do you know about the effects of alcohol on our bodies? Read the descriptions in the infographic below and give each a title from the box.

| Bladder | Bowel | Breasts (women) | Liver | Stomach |
| Blood pressure | Brain | Heart | Pancreas | |

### How Alcohol Affects Your Body (and how to avoid the side-effects)

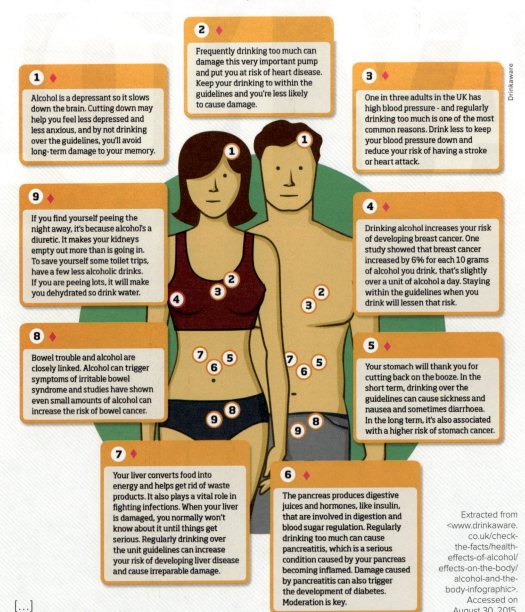

**1** ♦ Alcohol is a depressant so it slows down the brain. Cutting down may help you feel less depressed and less anxious, and by not drinking over the guidelines, you'll avoid long-term damage to your memory.

**2** ♦ Frequently drinking too much can damage this very important pump and put you at risk of heart disease. Keep your drinking to within the guidelines and you're less likely to cause damage.

**3** ♦ One in three adults in the UK has high blood pressure - and regularly drinking too much is one of the most common reasons. Drink less to keep your blood pressure down and reduce your risk of having a stroke or heart attack.

**4** ♦ Drinking alcohol increases your risk of developing breast cancer. One study showed that breast cancer increased by 6% for each 10 grams of alcohol you drink, that's slightly over a unit of alcohol a day. Staying within the guidelines when you drink will lessen that risk.

**5** ♦ Your stomach will thank you for cutting back on the booze. In the short term, drinking over the guidelines can cause sickness and nausea and sometimes diarrhoea. In the long term, it's also associated with a higher risk of stomach cancer.

**6** ♦ The pancreas produces digestive juices and hormones, like insulin, that are involved in digestion and blood sugar regulation. Regularly drinking too much can cause pancreatitis, which is a serious condition caused by your pancreas becoming inflamed. Damage caused by pancreatitis can also trigger the development of diabetes. Moderation is key.

**7** ♦ Your liver converts food into energy and helps get rid of waste products. It also plays a vital role in fighting infections. When your liver is damaged, you normally won't know about it until things get serious. Regularly drinking over the unit guidelines can increase your risk of developing liver disease and cause irreparable damage.

**8** ♦ Bowel trouble and alcohol are closely linked. Alcohol can trigger symptoms of irritable bowel syndrome and studies have shown even small amounts of alcohol can increase the risk of bowel cancer.

**9** ♦ If you find yourself peeing the night away, it's because alcohol's a diuretic. It makes your kidneys empty out more than is going in. To save yourself some toilet trips, have a few less alcoholic drinks. If you are peeing lots, it will make you dehydrated so drink water.

diarrhoea (UK)
diarrhea (US)

Drinkaware

Extracted from <www.drinkaware.co.uk/check-the-facts/health-effects-of-alcohol/effects-on-the-body/alcohol-and-the-body-infographic>. Accessed on August 30, 2015.

[...]

**2.** Where can you find detailed current data and analysis on issues such as alcohol consumption in your country or around the world? Choose the correct alternative.

- On blog posts.
- In travel tips articles.
- In songs.
- In survey and research reports.

Unit 7 Alcohol Consumption

# READING COMPREHENSION

## Before Reading

**1.** Look at the title of the report and answer: what specific issues regarding alcohol consumption do you think the survey report below will address?

> **TIP**
>
> Lembre-se de que suas experiências pessoais e seu conhecimento prévio sempre podem ajudá-lo a levantar hipóteses acerca do que você vai ler. Isso certamente facilitará a compreensão durante a leitura.

## Reading

behaviour (UK)
behavior (US)

### Alcohol Use 2012/13: New Zealand Health Survey

Published online: 4 February 2015

**Summary**

The alcohol use report presents the key findings from the 2012/13 New Zealand Health Survey about alcohol use, misuse and alcohol-related harm among New Zealand adults aged 15 years and over.

The following topics are covered:

- patterns of alcohol consumption
- alcohol use by pregnant women
- alcohol availability and use.

Separate publications will report the findings about the use of recreational drugs by New Zealand adults in 2012/13.

**Patterns of alcohol consumption**

- In 2012/13 most adults had consumed alcohol in the past 12 months, typically doing so in their home or in another's home. Most drinkers made a point of eating always or most of the time when they drank alcohol.
- A third of drinkers drank alcohol regularly: at least three to four times a week. Half of drinkers had drunk to intoxication at least once in the past 12 months, with a much smaller percentage reporting drinking to intoxication at least weekly.
- Drinkers reported a range of risky behaviours while drinking. Drinking and driving was most commonly reported, with one in six drinkers who drove in the past year having driven while feeling under the influence of alcohol.
- Drinkers experienced a range of harms as a result of their own drinking. Harm to physical health was the harm most commonly reported. A range of harms due to someone else's drinking were reported. Violent harms were the most commonly reported harm resulting from someone else's drinking.

**Alcohol use by pregnant women**

- In 2012/13 about one in five women who were pregnant in the last 12 months drank alcohol at some point during their most recent pregnancy. Of these women the majority reported past-year risky drinking.
- Most women who were pregnant in the last 12 months altered their drinking behaviour leading up to and during pregnancy. More than two-thirds of women who were pregnant in the last 12 months and who had ever drunk alcohol received advice not to drink during pregnancy.

**Alcohol availability and use**

- Alcohol outlets are within a short driving distance for most New Zealanders. Off-licence alcohol outlet density is greatest in the most deprived areas.
- Hazardous drinkers living within the most deprived urban areas are more likely to live within two minutes' drive of multiple off-licence alcohol outlets than hazardous drinkers living in the least deprived urban areas.

[...]

Extracted from <www.health.govt.nz/publication/alcohol-use-2012-13-new-zealand-health-survey>. Accessed on August 30, 2015.

**2.** Match the information to the words and expressions in the circle.

a. patterns of alcohol consumption; alcohol use by pregnant women; alcohol availability and use

b. analyze data and alert readers to alcohol-related harm and misuse

c. alcohol use, misuse and alcohol-related harm among New Zealand adults aged 15 years and over

d. 2012/2013

e. 15

**3.** In your notebook, write what the numbers below refer to.

a. 1/3.

b. 50%.

c. 3 or 4 times a week.

d. 1/5.

**TIP**

Procure identificar números, frações e porcentagens em um texto e, em seguida, descubra a que eles se referem. Essa estratégia facilitará a compreensão mais detalhada do que foi lido.

**4.** Write T (True) or F (False). Go back to the text on page 115, if necessary.

a. No report about drug use has been done.

b. Most adults drank at home or at another's home.

c. Almost half of drinkers reported drinking to intoxication at least once a week.

d. Drinking and driving was one of the risky behaviors acknowledged by drinkers.

e. Five in six drinkers drank and drove in the twelve months.

**5.** Match the false sentences in the previous activity to the parts which correct them. There is one extra part.

1. Separate publications will report the findings about the use of recreational drugs by New Zealand adults in 2012/13.

2. Alcohol outlets are within a short driving distance for most New Zealanders. Off-licence alcohol outlet density is greatest in the most deprived areas.

3. Half of drinkers had drunk to intoxication at least once in the past 12 months […]

4. Drinking and driving was most commonly reported, with one in six drinkers who drove in the past year having driven while feeling under the influence of alcohol.

116  Unit 7  Alcohol Consumption

**6.** Answer the questions below.

   **a.** Is there any information in this report that surprised you, or did you already know all this? Explain your answer.

   **b.** Who commissioned this survey? Why do you think it was done?

   **c.** What are the consequences of alcohol intoxication beyond personal health issues? Justify your answer.

**7.** Read an extract about alcohol use in pregnancy. Then identify the effects alcohol consumption has on babies and their mothers.

> **Alcohol Use in Pregnancy**
>
> There is no known safe amount of alcohol use during pregnancy or while trying to get pregnant. There is also no safe time during pregnancy to drink. All types of alcohol are equally harmful, including all wines and beer. When a pregnant woman drinks alcohol, so does her baby. [...]

Extracted from <www.cdc.gov/ncbddd/fasd/alcohol-use.html>. Accessed on March 27, 2016.

> **TIP**
> Use seu conhecimento de mundo para refletir sobre assuntos que ainda não sejam de seu total domínio. Troque ideias e esteja aberto para novas descobertas e informações.

   **a.** It increases the risk of miscarriage and stillbirth.

   **b.** The baby might be underweight at birth and have learning disabilities.

   **c.** The baby might grow slowly after birth.

   **d.** The baby could have heart, bones, or kidney disease.

   **e.** The baby might have a poor memory.

**8.** Find the only characteristic that doesn't belong to survey reports.

   **a.** They are based on research.

   **b.** They present information about when and how the data was collected.

   **c.** Subheadings can be used to separate each piece of information.

   **d.** They always describe plans to conduct a future survey about the same topic.

   **e.** Percentages and proportions are commonly used as well as expressions such as *half of, one in half of, most of*.

   **f.** They present a summary in their opening paragraph.

## After Reading

- In your opinion, what is the worst aspect of alcohol abuse?
- Have you ever heard about support groups for heavy drinkers or drug addicts? What do you think these support groups do?

# VOCABULARY STUDY

**1.** Some words may express different ideas depending on the context they are in. The passages below belong to the survey report on page 115. Choose the correct meaning of the words in bold.

> **TIP**
> Reconhecer os diferentes sentidos de uma palavra de acordo com seu contexto vai ajudá-lo(a) na compreensão de textos.

a. "The alcohol use report presents the **key** findings from the 2012/13 New Zealand Health Survey about alcohol use".
- a small piece of shaped metal with incisions cut to fit the wards of a particular lock, and that is inserted into a lock and turned to open or close it
- each of several buttons on a panel for operating a computer, typewriter, or telephone
- of paramount or crucial importance

b. "**patterns** of alcohol consumption"
- a regular and intelligible form or sequence discernible in certain actions or situations
- a repeated decorative design
- a wooden or metal model from which a mold is made for a casting

c. Most drinkers made a **point** of eating always or most of the time when they drank alcohol."
- a dot or other punctuation mark, in particular a period
- an argument or idea put forward by a person in a discussion
- a particular spot, place, or position in an area or on a map, object, or surface

d. "Drinkers experienced a range of harms as a result of their **own** drinking."
- admit or acknowledge that something is the case or that one feels a certain way
- have (something) as one's own; possess
- someone or something that belongs or relates to the person mentioned

Adapted from <www.oxforddictionaries.com/us>. Accessed on August 30, 2015.

**2.** Read the extract below and complete the sentence that follows.

> **TIP**
> Reconhecer as palavras de uma mesma família vai ajudá-lo(a) a ampliar seu vocabulário.

> "Most women who were pregnant in the last 12 months altered their drinking behaviour leading up to and during pregnancy."

In English, word families are groups of words which are firmly related to one another, either in form or in meaning. In the extract above, two words that belong to the same word family are ♦ and ♦.

**3.** Come up with two word families related to the theme of this unit. Find at least three words belonging to each family and write them down in your notebook. Then write sentences contextualizing some of them.

Unit 7  Alcohol Consumption

# LANGUAGE IN CONTEXT

## Passive Voice I

1. Read three extracts from the survey report on page 115 and identify all the verb forms. Then decide whether the statements are T (True) or F (False) and correct the false ones in your notebook.

    I. "The alcohol use report presents the key findings from the 2012/13 New Zealand Health Survey about alcohol use…"

    II. "The following topics are covered…"

    III. "Drinking and driving was most commonly reported, with one in six drinkers…"

    a. In extracts II and III it's not possible to know who or what performed the action.

    b. The subjects of extracts I, II, and III are the receivers of the actions.

    c. Extracts II and III focus on what or who performs the actions and not on the actions themselves.

2. Now complete the sentences about the extracts in activity 1.

    a. In extracts ♦ and ♦, the importance of the agent performing the action is reduced. Those statements are in the Passive Voice. In the Passive Voice, sometimes we do not know who or what performed the action, and its agent may not even be mentioned.

    b. The ♦ Voice is mostly used in writing and is often formal and impersonal. The ♦ Voice, on the other hand, is usually clearer and easier to understand.

3. Read the statements below and match the columns to form meaningful sentences about the formation of the Passive Voice.

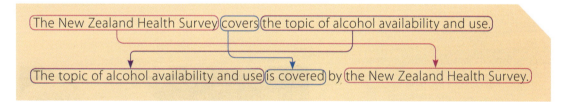

   a. The object of the Active Voice statement
   b. The subject of the Active Voice statement
   c. In the Passive Voice, the agent
   d. The verb to be in the same tense of the main verb of the Active Voice

   - becomes the agent in the Passive Voice statement.
   - is followed by the past participle of that verb in the Passive Voice.
   - becomes the subject of the Passive Voice statement.
   - is introduced by the preposition *by*.

> Observe que a formação da voz passiva em língua inglesa assemelha-se à formação da voz passiva em língua portuguesa.

4. Read the statements below about the survey report on page 115. Find the verb forms and write AV if they are in the Active Voice or PV if they are in the Passive Voice.

   a. The New Zealand Health Survey was published online on February 2015.

   b. Key findings from the 2012/13 New Zealand Health Survey are presented in the report.

   c. The report covers issues such as patterns of alcohol consumption and alcohol availability and use, for example.

   d. One in three drinkers drank alcohol at least three to four times a week.

   e. A range of risky behaviours behind the wheel was reported by drinkers.

5. Read the text and use the present or the past passive forms of the verbs from the box to complete it.

   | arrest | bring | find | fine | intoxicate |

   ### Drunk Driving Fines Increased: Daily

   By Contributing Reporter on December 23, 2012
   By Ben Tavener, Senior Contributing Reporter

   RIO DE JANEIRO, BRAZIL – A major anti-drinking and driving operation by Rio police has led to over 150 motorists being fined after new legislation ♦ into effect. Of 1,800 drivers stopped, 153 failed breathalyzer tests on the first night of stricter rules of the *Lei Seca* (literally "Dry Law") – some ♦ also ♦ after refusing to cooperate with officers, according to local government sources.

   [...]

   Those who ♦ to be over the limit ♦ and had their license seized. The new rules came into force on Friday, December 21st, and carry a considerably larger fine: R$1,915 (US$921) up from R$957.

   [...]

   Even if someone refuses to take a breathalyzer test – which is how drivers used to try to escape being fined or arrested, police may now charge motorists if they ♦ visibly ♦, and have the right to use proof collected at the scene, including video recordings, as supporting evidence.

   [...]

   Those caught drinking-and-driving in Brazil now face a fine of R$1,915 (US$921), image recreation.

   Adapted from <riotimesonline.com/brazil-news/rio-politics/drunk-driving-law-fines-increased-in-brazil/#>.
   Accessed on January 30, 2016.

Unit 7 Alcohol Consumption

6. Read the text and choose the correct verb forms to complete it. Write the answers in your notebook.

### First arrests made under new Fukuoka drunk driving regulations

**Sep. 23, 2012 - 06:05AM JST**

FUKUOKA – Police said Saturday that two men arrested in Fukuoka on Friday are the first suspects to be arrested under the prefecture's new, harsher penalties for drunk driving offenses.

The new penalties are part of a long-term plan to eradicate the practise of driving under the influence of alcohol in the prefecture, Sankei Shimbun reported.

Fukuoka Prefecture has been running a high-profile anti-drunk driving campaign since August 2006, when a 22-year-old man ♦ his vehicle into the back of an SUV containing a family of five. The collision ♦ the SUV through a bridge railing, and the vehicle plunged into Hakata Bay. The two parents survived with minor injuries, but their three children, aged 4, 3 and 1, died.

Further initiatives ♦ to raise awareness of the dangers of drunk driving. In May 2012, all Fukuoka city employees ♦ to abstain from drinking any alcohol for a month by Mayor Soichiro Takashima, after a scandal involving two city officials.

In August, Fukuoka Prefecture announced a comprehensive drunk driving prevention plan that aims to eliminate the number of traffic accidents caused by drunk drivers. The new plan, based on the prefectural government ordinance on elimination of drunk driving, means that drivers arrested for driving under the influence ♦ to attend programs and watch videos designed to deter future offenses.

The plan also ♦ educational institutions, such as schools and universities, to discourage acceptance of underage drinking and help prevent drunk driving.

[…]

Adapted from <www.japantoday.com/smartphone/view/crime/first-arrests-made-under-new-fukuoka-drunk-driving-regulations>. Accessed on January 30, 2016.

a. was driven • drove
b. was pushed • pushed
c. were tested • tested
d. were ordered • ordered
e. are obliged • oblige
f. is urged • urges

practise (UK)
practice (US)

7. In your notebook, rewrite the message from the poster in the Passive Voice.

Extracted from <manninglive.com/2015/06/25/dnr-dont-drink-and-boat>. Accessed on September 2, 2015.

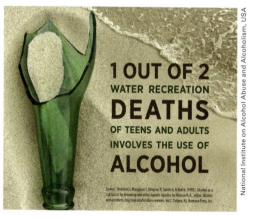

## WRAPPING UP

In pairs, refer back to the infographic on page 114 and write two sentences in your notebook about how our bodies **are affected** by alcohol. Do not forget to use the Passive Voice in the Simple Present. Then read your sentences to the class.

# LISTENING COMPREHENSION

## Before Listening

1. Read the first paragraph of the recording you are about to hear. What do you think the recording is about? Discuss with the whole group.

> Did you know that 41% of kids have had at least one alcoholic drink by the age of 14 or that 2.6 million teens don't know that you can die from an alcoholic overdose?

## Listening

2. Listen and check if your prediction was correct.

3. Listen to the first statements in Kaitlyn Stoneburner's report on underage drinking and pick out the wrong information. Then correct the sentences in your notebook.

> O NIAAA (*National Institute on Alcohol Abuse and Alcoholism*) é parte integrante dos NIH (*National Institutes of Health*), agência governamental norte-americana que tem como objetivo patrocinar e conduzir pesquisas sobre o impacto do consumo de álcool na saúde e no bem-estar do ser humano.

   a. Boys usually start drinking alcohol at the age of 13.

   b. 45% of people who begin drinking before the age of 16 become dependent on alcohol at some point in their lives.

   c. Most teens never drink more than five drinks at a time.

   d. Binge drinking can cause heart disease, but it cannot cause a coma or death.

   e. Alcohol can damage a few organs in our body.

4. Now listen to the second part of the recording and answer the following questions.

   a. When did Natasha start drinking?

   b. How much was she drinking by the age of 13?

   c. What happened to her when she was 14?

   d. Natasha is 18 now and she still feels the consequences of alcohol consumption. What kind of consequences are they?

5. Complete the sentences. Then refer to the transcript on page 186 and check your answers.

   a. People who hang around drinkers take a great risk of being ♦ and ♦.

   b. About 7000 people under the age of 21 ♦ from alcohol-related injuries.

   c. 66% of the teens interviewed said that ♦.

   d. Underage drinking is also common in ♦, not just big cities.

Unit 7 Alcohol Consumption

## After Listening

**6.** In pairs, discuss: what is the purpose of this recording? Justify.

### PRONUNCIATION PRACTICE

Listen and repeat the words below. Then find the words that have the sound /aɪ/.

| big | high | since |
|---|---|---|
| die | kid | time |
| drink | liver | violence |
| figure | lives | visit |
| give | risk | with |

# SPEAKING

The map below shows the minimum legal drinking age in 190 countries. In pairs, look at the map and then answer the following questions.

✓ Is alcohol banned anywhere? Where? Why do you think that is?
✓ In how many countries can people start drinking legally between the ages 18 and 19?
✓ Is there any country where there is no legal drinking age?
✓ From your point of view, should there be a legal drinking age in all countries or not? If so, what age should this be? If not, why?

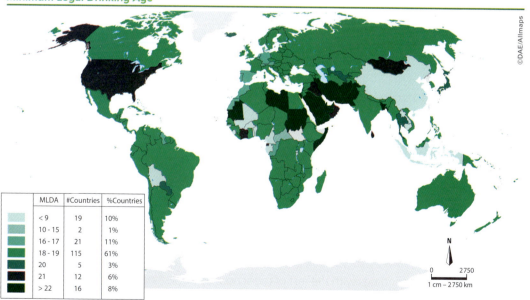

Minimum Legal Drinking Age

| MLDA | #Countries | %Countries |
|---|---|---|
| < 9 | 19 | 10% |
| 10 - 15 | 2 | 1% |
| 16 - 17 | 21 | 11% |
| 18 - 19 | 115 | 61% |
| 20 | 5 | 3% |
| 21 | 12 | 6% |
| > 22 | 16 | 8% |

Adapted from <drinkingage.procon.org/view.resource.php?resourceID=004294>.
Accessed on September 4, 2015.

Alcohol Consumption **Unit 7**

# WRITING

In small groups, do a survey among the people in your school on an agreed topic and write a report to share your friends.

## Planning your survey report

- Talk to your classmate and decide on the topic you are interested in writing a report about.
- Do some research on the Internet about the topic you have chosen.
- Design a survey and include questions that will help you to obtain relevant information for writing the report.
- Make sure your questions are clear and your interviewees can understand them.
- Do the survey among people in your school. Then collect and organize all the information.

## Writing and rewriting your text

- Write a draft of your survey report in your notebook.

---

**REFLECTING AND EVALUATING**

Go back to your survey report and make sure you paid attention to the following topics:

✓ Did you chose a title?

✓ Does your report present a summary in the opening paragraph?

✓ Did you mention percentages and proportions to make the report clearer?

✓ Is the collected data analyzed correctly?

---

- Before asking the teacher for correction, read the report and revise it.
- Make all the necessary adjustments and write a clean copy.

## After writing

- Arrange the desks in the classroom in a u-shape to make it easier to discuss your reports with the whole class.
- Read your report aloud and listen to your classmates' reports. Then exchange opinions and points of view.
- Share your findings with the rest of the school by publishing your report on the school website.

# SELF-ASSESSMENT

Chegamos ao fim da unidade 7. Convidamos você a refletir sobre seu desempenho até aqui e responder às questões propostas abaixo, escolhendo uma das seguintes opções:

> Sim.

> Preciso me preparar mais.

### Questões

- Você reúne argumentos suficientes para expor e defender, de maneira clara e coerente, sua opinião em relação ao consumo de bebidas alcoólicas e os prejuízos que elas causam em nosso organismo?
- Você está apto a ler e compreender diferentes relatórios de pesquisa e reconhecer as características principais inerentes ao gênero?
- Você reúne conhecimentos linguístico-discursivos para produzir um relatório de pesquisa em inglês?
- Você está preparado para escutar anúncios para dependentes de bebidas alcoólicas e compreender informações específicas?
- Você se julga apto a analisar dados em um mapa e discutir sobre eles?

### Refletindo sobre suas respostas

- Como você analisa a evolução do seu aprendizado em relação à unidade anterior?
- De que forma suas práticas de aprendizagem no decorrer desta unidade influenciaram suas respostas?
- O que você pode fazer para aprimorar ainda mais os conhecimentos adquiridos nesta unidade?

    a. Buscar por mais informações sobre o comportamento dos adolescentes em relação ao consumo de bebidas alcoólicas em diferentes sociedades.
    b. Ler mais relatórios de pesquisa e observar as estruturas linguísticas e lexicais comumente usadas nesse gênero textual.
    c. Aprofundar meus conhecimentos em língua inglesa, usando recursos diversos, de forma que minha participação nas atividades seja mais ativa.
    d. Outros.

# UNIT 8

# CHILD PROTECTION

**Nesta unidade você terá oportunidade de:**

- entender a situação do trabalho infantil ao redor do mundo;

- reconhecer os objetivos e algumas das características dos resumos de relatórios e produzir;

- compreender o áudio de um vídeo sobre a história do trabalho infantil;

- refletir e discutir sobre o que pode ser feito para combater a exploração infantil.

- Que relação podemos estabelecer entre a imagem e o título da unidade?
- Como podemos interpretar a posição da criança?

127

# STARTING OUT

 Geography History

1. Look at the pictures. What do they portray?

2. Now match the pictures to the passages below and find out what each is about.

- Assisted by her mother, Masha, 5, laughs as she practices walking in her new body brace, at the Ukrainian Research Institute for Prosthetic Design and Rehabilitation in the eastern city of Kharkiv. Masha was born with spastic cerebral palsy, a form of impaired muscle movement caused by injury to the brain during foetal development or birth.

    Extracted from <www.unicef.org/protection/57929_58537.html?p=printme>. Accessed on September 2, 2015.

- A young boy is helped by his teacher to learn how to use a computer at a primary school in Wisconsin, US, 2015.

    Extracted from http://www.unicef.org/protection/57929_79672.html. Accessed on September 2, 2015.

- Shaquila Raimundo, 10, registers herself during community birth-registration activities at Puzuzu Primary School in Maganja da Costa District in Zambézia Province.

    Extracted from <www.unicef.org/protection/57929_58010.html>. Accessed on March 24, 2016.

3. Work in pairs to answer the questions below.

- Would you be interested in reading a summary of a report on violence against children? Why/Why not?

- What other summary reports would you be interested in reading? Justify your answer.

128  Unit 8  Child Protection

# READING COMPREHENSION

## Before Reading

**1.** Skim the summary report below and answer: what do the numbers in blue refer to?

## Reading

### What is this report about?

All children in the country have the right to be protected from abuse, violence and things that could harm them. The Bill of Rights in the Constitution of South Africa makes this very clear and so do the laws of the country, such as the Children's Act and Child Justice Act.

The Government is very serious about the protection of all children in the country, and that is why they wrote this report on why children experience violence and abuse. When we know why children are victims of abuse and violence, we will be able to make better plans to ensure it stops.

### Violence against children
# IN SOUTH AFRICA

There are many reasons for the high levels of violence in South Africa. The violence is partly due to the years of apartheid which caused big differences between people living in the country. We also know that alcohol and drug abuse cause people to behave violently and hurt others, especially children.

Police statistics show that in 2011/2012 (a period of one year) a total of 50,688 children were victims of violent crimes in South Africa. Below are some details on the kinds of violent crimes committed against children for this period:

* 793 children were murdered.
* 758 children were victims of attempted murder.
* 25,862 children were victims of sexual offences against them.
* 12,645 children were victims of common assault.
* 10,630 children were victims of assault with grievous bodily harm.

We also know that many crimes against children, especially violent crimes, are not always reported to the police. There are many reasons for violent crime not being reported but often it is because:

* The child is too young to report the crime (or tell someone what happened).
* Children are afraid to speak up because they fear the criminal.
* Children are unsure of what will happen when they report the crime (or tell someone what happened).
* Children don't know where to report the crime.

It is important that the Government and other organisations working with children have up-to-date numbers of children who are victims of abuse and violence to help them:

* Plan better for the future.
* Introduce the right services to support children.
* Start projects to stop the high levels of violence in particular areas.

Department of Women, Children and People with Disabilities and UNICEF, 2013

Child Protection **Unit 8**  129

## Violence against children
# IN TROUBLE WITH THE LAW

The Child Justice Act is a special law that deals with children who clash with the law (commit a crime). It provides protection for children who are alleged to have committed a crime, or who have been found guilty of committing a crime.

If you are younger than 18 years, you should be treated differently to adults who have committed a crime. Children may also not be held in cells with adults, and boys and girls must be kept separately. This helps to prevent abuse and violence against children.

Sometimes children who are detained are treated badly or become victims of violence, either caused by other children or adults who are the perpetrators. Special measures need to be put in place to ensure this does not happen, or when it happens children should be able to report incidents and get services to support them.

Extracted from <www.unicef.org/southafrica/resources_16010.html>. Accessed on November 28, 2015.

**2.** What is the purpose of this summary report?

   a. To summarize how complex it is to define violence in South Africa.

   b. To provide people with important information about violence and abuse against children in South Africa.

   c. To expose some important penal code articles that punish anyone who disrespects children's rights.

   d. To teach parents how to prevent child abuse.

**3.** Write T (True), F (False) or NM (Not Mentioned).

   a. Violence against children is more like to happen in poor families.

   b. The summary report bears information regarding children's rights.

   c. Police statistics regarding violence against children in South Africa are always accurate.

   d. When children are held in cells with adults, they can be victims of crimes.

   e. Mistreatment of children is a global problem with serious life-long consequences for its victims.

   f. Many young children are abused by larger or older children.

**4.** Rewrite correctly the sentence(s) that you have checked as false in the previous activity. Use your own words.

**5.** Read one more extract of the summary report Violence Against Children in South Africa. Then answer the questions.

> **Violence against chidren in school**
> Children spend a lot of time in school; some can spend up to 12 years of their childhood in school. Therefore, adults (such as teachers) working in schools have a duty to ensure that children are safe and protected during the school day. Unfortunately, many children do not feel safe in their schools and may experience some form of violence. A 2008 study showed that about 1,8 million children (15 percent of all learners) experienced some form of violence while at school. This violence is usually carried out by:
> * Other children in the school of the same age (peers) or older children
> * Adults in the school, for example teachers.
> [...]

Extracted from <www.unicef.org/southafrica/SAF_resources_violenceagainstchildren.pdf>. Accessed on March 28, 2016.

  a. In your opinion, what forms of violence do South African children experience in school?

  b. What do you think could be done to avoid these problems?

**6.** In pairs, discuss the questions below. Then write down your answers and share them with the whole class.

  a. This summary report was written for teens. Why do you think UNICEF South Africa write this summary report for them?

  b. Looking at the reasons that children don't report abuses, what could be done to help them to come forward and speak out against their abuser(s)? Explain your answer.

  c. Do you notice any similarities between the information presented in this summary report and the situation in Brazil? Justify your answer.

**7.** Identify some characteristics of summary reports.

  a. Summary reports tell the titles of the reports.

  b. They try to give accurate and objective information about the topic.

  c. They shorten the main parts of the report.

  d. Authors of summary reports present personal opinions.

  e. They sometimes use images and graphs to make the information clearer.

  f. They defend a position or opinion.

  g. The author's own voice is used to convey the message.

## After Reading

- Jeroo Billimoria, an Indian social entrepreneur, says, "Children need systems that are inclusive and driven by them, systems that will enable them to respond to their feelings and needs at any time."

  Extracted from <www.ashoka.org/fellow/jeroo-billimoria>. Accessed on November 15, 2015.

- Have you ever felt as if your feelings and needs weren't considered when a decision regarding your life was being made? Justify your answer.

- Do you think that the educational system can help to guarantee children's rights? Explain.

# VOCABULARY STUDY

1. Refer back to the text on pages 129 and 130 to infer the meaning of the words from the box. Next, use them to complete the extract from UNICEF's Child Protection Information Sheet *What is Child Protection*?

    > abuse   law   protection   right   violence

    **programme** (UK)
    **program** (US)

    UNICEF uses the term 'child protection' to refer to preventing and responding to ♦ exploitation and abuse against children — including commercial sexual exploitation, trafficking, child labour and harmful traditional practices, such as female genital mutilation/cutting and child marriage. UNICEF's child ♦ programmes also target children who are uniquely vulnerable to these abuses, such as when living without parental care, in conflict with the ♦ and in armed conflict. Violations of the child's ♦ to protection take place in every country and are massive, under-recognized and under-reported barriers to child survival and development, in addition to being human rights violations. Children subjected to violence, exploitation, ♦ and neglect are at risk of death, poor physical and mental health, HIV/AIDS infection, educational problems, displacement, homelessness, vagrancy and poor parenting skills later in life. […]

    Extracted from <www.unicef.org/protection/files/What_is_Child_Protection.pdf>. Accessed on November 29, 2015.

2. Read the text on pages 129 and 130, find an example of a compound adjective formed from a phrase, and write it down in your notebook.

3. Match the compound adjectives to their corresponding definitions. Then use one of them to complete the passage below.

    a. up-to-date
    b. down-to-earth
    c. out-of-date
    d. on-the-job
    e. long-drawn-out

    • happening during one's work
    • extending to the present time
    • gone out of style or fashion
    • lasting a very long time
    • practical and realistic

    Adapted from <dictionary.reference.com/>. Accessed on November 29, 2015.

    > […]
    >
    > **Child protection procedures**
    >
    > These procedures are now fully web-based. If you need to print these procedures out (for example, for a meeting), please only print the relevant section. If you do print a section out please be aware that this is only valid for 72 hours as they are regularly updated and you may be using ♦ guidance if you refer back to previous versions. Always refer to the website for the most current version.
    >
    > […]

    Extracted from <www.gateshead.gov.uk/lscb/Child-protection-procedures/OurProcedures.aspx>. Accessed on November 29, 2015.

# LANGUAGE IN CONTEXT

## Passive Voice II

1. Read the extracts from the summary report on pages 129 and 130 and identify the ones in the Passive Voice.

   a. "793 children were murdered"

   b. "Children are afraid to speak up because they fear the criminal"

   c. "This helps to prevent abuse and violence against children"

   d. "Children may also not be held in cells with adults, and boys and girls must be kept separately"

   e. "758 children were victims of attempted murder".

2. Find the only statement that is NOT correct about the Passive Voice.

   a. The object of the active statement becomes the subject in the passive voice.

   b. We do not use the verb *to be* in the passive voice.

   c. Modal verbs are followed by the infinitive form of the verb *to be* and the past participle of the main verb from the active voice statement.

   For more information about the Passive Voice, go to Language Reference, pages 179 and 180.

3. Use the cues to form Passive Voice statements and write them down in your notebook. Remember to change the verb forms.

   a. All children in South Africa / must protect / from abuse, violence and things that could harm them

   b. Crimes against children / should report / to the police

   c. Children / may abuse / if they remain in cells with adults

   d. Children who are detained / might treat badly / or become victims of violence

   e. Incidents in detention / must account for formally

   f. Those who are younger than 18 years of age / should regard differently / from adults who have committed a crime

**4.** Read the text and choose the best alternative to complete it.

### THEN AND NOW
#### Alyssa and Deanna

When Alyssa and Deanna ♦ in a cardboard box in the bogs of New Jersey, their skin was caked with dirt. All but two of 3-year-old Deanna's teeth were completely decayed, and 7-month-old Alyssa's neck muscles were so underdeveloped that she ♦ her head. The girls ♦, and put in a temporary foster home. But a year later, the state ♦ no viable plan to place the sisters in a permanent family.

Only after CR ♦ a reform campaign in New Jersey and named Alyssa and Deanna as plaintiffs were the girls finally moved to an adoptive home. Now, they are thriving under the love and care of their family. [...]

Extracted from <www.childrensrights.org/our-kids/then-and-now/>. Accessed on May 23, 2016.

**a.** found / couldn't hold up / were rescued / should have / began

**b.** found / couldn't be held up / was rescued / had / began

**c.** were found / couldn't hold up / were rescued / had / began

**d.** were found / couldn't hold up / was rescued / must have / begins

**5.** Complete the text below by writing the words in parentheses in the correct order. Write the complete sentences in your notebook.

### In five years: two children abandoned by their parents
[...]

Miriam Dalli 19 November 2012, 12:00am

Over the past five years, ♦ (in / two / their / abandoned / Malta / were / children / by / parents). ♦ (Minister / the / by / information / Justice / revealed / was) Chris Said in reply to a question raised by Labour MP Carmelo Abela.

According to Agenzija Appogg, an 'abandoned' child refers to those cases where the parents would be untraceable. The child would have been listed as being in the care of the parents.

Minister Said revealed that the two children were abandoned in Cospicua and Rabat. ♦ (the / cases / involved / both / in / Police / was).

"The two minors are today protected by a protection order," he added.

Extracted from <www.maltatoday.com.mt/news/national/22771/in-five-years-two-children-abandoned-by-their-parents-20121119#.VenRtflVhHw>. Accessed on September 4, 2015.

Unit 8 Child Protection

**6.** Read an extract from the fact sheet *The right to participation* and complete it with the Passive Voice of the verbs from the box.

> [...]
> **Participation is the path to other rights**
>
> The right to participation is relevant to the exercise of all other rights, within the family, the school and the larger community context.
>
> Thus, for example:
>
> - **Adoption**. As one of "the persons concerned," the child ♦ in any judicial or administrative adoption proceedings. Article 21(a) refers to the informed consent of persons concerned, including the child.
> - **Separation from parents**. In decisions to be taken on the need to separate a child from his or her parents (for example, on the basis of abuse or neglect), the child - as an "interested party" – ♦ an opportunity to participate and make his or her views known.
> - **Name change**. In a decision to be taken on the changing of a child's name, the views of the child ♦ into consideration.
> - **Right to health**. Children are entitled to be informed, have access to information and be supported in the use of basic knowledge of child health and nutrition (article 24(2)e) so that they may enjoy their right to health.
> - **Education**. [...] In brief, the right to education means the right to experience citizenship. To achieve citizenship and all it entails, children ♦ not as mere recipients of knowledge, but rather as active players in the learning process.
>
> [...]

must give
must perceive
should hear
should take

Extracted from <www.unicef.org/crc/files/Right-to-Participation.pdf>.
Accessed on September 4, 2015.

**7.** Take a closer look at the passive voice statements in the previous activity and answer this question in your notebook: why was the Passive Voice used?

### WRAPPING UP

In pairs, exchange ideas about children's rights and complete the sentences below. Make sure to use passive voice statements. Then share your sentences with your classmates and listen to theirs as well.

From our point of view:
- Children shouldn't be ♦
- Children must be ♦
- Children could be ♦
- Children can't be ♦

Child Protection **Unit 8**  135

# LISTENING COMPREHENSION

## Before Listening

**1.** Look at the following images. What do you think you will listen about?

## Listening

 **2.** Listen to the recording and check if your prediction was correct.

**3.** Listen to the recording again and answer these specific questions.

   a. Why were children used as laborers in the early 1900s?

   b. How old were Furman Owes and other children when they started working in a South Carolina mill?

   c. Why didn't he and the others go to school at that time?

   d. What did individual workers and social reformers fight against in the 1800s and 1900s?

   e. Who brought child labor to an end in the United States?

## After Listening

Read the extract below and discuss the following question with your classmates: Why didn't the strikes solve the problem at that time?

> "Striking was an effective bargaining tool. But going on strike was not just a parade. It was more like a rebellion, and the situation could be terrifying and dangerous. Local and national governments treated strikes as civil unrest and often dispatched armed troops to break them up. Workers were injured, and many died as they clashed police and National Guard."

## SPEAKING

In small groups:

- ✓ Prepare a picture-based slide presentation about the Brazilian history of child labor. You can research about it in magazines, books, or on the Internet. You can talk to your History teacher as well.
- ✓ Take notes and look for pictures that illustrate the topic.
- ✓ Show the pictures to your teacher and tell him/her what you want to talk about.
- ✓ Present the slides to your classmates.

# WRITING

In pairs, write a summary report to present to your classmates.

## Planning your summary report

- Do some research on reports on the Internet and choose the one you consider the most interesting to summarize and present to your classmates.
- You can research reports about:
  - gender disparities;
  - entrepreneurship;
  - careers of the future;
  - technology, and social media, among others.
- Read the report several times to better understand the issue.
- Label each paragraph with a sentence that sums up its contents.
- Highlight and take notes of all the relevant information on a separate sheet of paper.

## Writing and rewriting your text

- Write a draft of your summary report in your notebook.
- Ask a pair of classmates to read your summary report and give their opinion about it.
- Make all the necessary adjustments and write a clean copy.

### REFLECTING AND EVALUATING

Go back to your summary report and make sure you paid attention to the following topics:

- ✓ Did you include the title, the author, and the date of the original text?
- ✓ Does the summary report present the main ideas of the source?
- ✓ Did you leave out all personal views and inferences?
- ✓ Did you check your summary report against the original source for accuracy?
- ✓ Is there a logical flow of ideas?
- ✓ Is the issue attractive to the readers?
- ✓ Are your grammar, punctuation, and spelling correct?

## After writing

- Present your summary report to your classmates so you can discuss the topic.
- Alternatively, you can publish the summary report on the school website or blog.

# SELF-ASSESSMENT

Chegamos ao fim da unidade 8. Convidamos você a refletir sobre seu desempenho até aqui e responder às questões propostas abaixo, escolhendo uma das seguintes opções:

Sim.

Preciso me preparar mais.

### Questões

- Você tem conhecimento suficiente para expor sua opinião acerca do trabalho infantil ao redor do mundo?
- Você se sente capaz de ler e compreender resumos de relatórios em língua inglesa e reconhecer as características principais inerentes ao gênero?
- Você reúne conhecimentos linguístico-discursivos suficientes para redigir um resumo de relatório em língua inglesa?
- Você está preparado para escutar e compreender áudio de vídeos sobre a história do trabalho infantil?
- Você se julga apto a expor e defender seu ponto de vista sobre o que pode ser feito para combater a exploração infantil?

### Refletindo sobre suas respostas

- Como você analisa a evolução do seu aprendizado em relação à unidade anterior?
- De que forma suas práticas de aprendizagem no decorrer desta unidade influenciaram suas respostas?
- O que você pode fazer para aprimorar ainda mais os conhecimentos adquiridos nesta unidade?
    a. Buscar por mais informações sobre a exploração infantil ao redor do mundo, bem como sobre as medidas de prevenção e/ou de solução que estão sendo tomadas em diferentes sociedades.
    b. Ler diferentes resumos de relatórios em língua inglesa e identificar os elementos linguísticos e lexicais mais comumente usados.
    c. Aprofundar meus conhecimentos em língua inglesa, usando recursos diversos, de forma que minha participação nas atividades seja mais ativa.
    d. Outros.

## Further Practice 4 – Units 7 & 8

1. Read the survey report and answer: does Dr. Michael Livingston have a positive or negative view of alcohol consumption by young Australians? Copy the part that justifies your answer.

### Young Aussie binge drinking in decline

15 July 2015

A new study examining Australian drinking patterns has identified a decline in underage binge drinking and an increase in the age at which many young people first drink alcohol.

It found the number of Australians aged between 14 and 17 who are binge drinking has decreased by half over the last 13 years, while the number of abstainers has more than doubled.

Funded by the Foundation for Alcohol Research and Education (FARE) and undertaken by the Centre for Alcohol Policy Research (CAPR) the study, *Understanding recent trends in Australian alcohol consumption*, draws insights from five waves of the Australian Institute of Health and Welfare's National Drug Strategy Household Survey (2001 to 2013) involving more than 120,000 respondents.

While rates of heavy drinking have remained stable among young adults (18-29), and have even increased among Australia's older populations, it is the youngest cohort (14-17) who have most markedly reduced their risk of alcohol-related harm.

The current 2013 data shows 5.1 per cent of 14-17 year olds reported drinking 20 or more standard drinks in a session at least once in the last 12 months, down from ten per cent in 2001.

Similarly, the proportion of Australians aged 14-17 who had consumed five or more standard drinks on an occasion has also halved, from 41.8 per cent down to 19.8 per cent over the same period.

Report author Dr. Michael Livingston was encouraged to see such promising trends. "Young people have sharply reduced their drinking over the last decade; in particular Australian teenagers are drinking less alcohol, and in less risky quantities," Dr. Livingston said.

More than half (57.3 per cent) of Australians aged between 14 and 17 are abstaining from drinking alcohol altogether, compared to 28 per cent in 2001.

[...]

Extracted from <www.fare.org.au/2015/07/young-aussie-binge-drinking-in-decline>. Accessed on September 3, 2015.

**2.** Read the sentences and write YES, NO, or NM (Not Mentioned) in your notebook.

   **a.** The number of people between 14 and 17 who are binge drinkers has declined substantially over the years.

   **b.** The number of abstainers has declined, too.

   **c.** Underage drinking is declining following worldwide trends.

   **d.** In 2001, only 5.1% reported drinking 20 or more standard drinks in a session.

**3.** Answer the questions. Give full answers.

   **a.** Who published the survey report?

   **b.** According to the survey report, which rates have remained steady?

   **c.** Which age group seems to be the most neglectful about alcohol consumption? Why?

**4.** Read the text and answer the questions that follow.

> ### Peer pressure can be good, too.
>
> Peer pressure isn't all bad. You and your friends can pressure each other into some things that will improve your health and social life and make you feel good about your decisions.
>
> Think of a time when a friend pushed you to do something good for yourself or to avoid something that would've been bad.
>
> **Here are some good things friends can pressure each other to do:**
>
> - Be honest
> - Avoid alcohol
> - Avoid drugs
> - Not smoke
> - Be nice
> - Respect others
> - Work hard
> - Exercise (together!)
>
> You and your friends can also use good peer pressure to help each other resist bad peer pressure.
>
> **If you see a friend taking some heat, try some of these lines ...**
>
> - We don't want to drink.
> - We don't need to drink to have fun.
> - Let's go and do something else.
> - Leave her alone. She said she didn't want any.

Extracted from <www.thecoolspot.gov/peer_pressure6.aspx>.
Accessed on January 31, 2016.

   **a.** Have you ever put pressure on your friends? If so, why? Share the experience with the whole class. If not, in what circumstances would you do it? Explain.

   **b.** In your opinion, how can we resist negative peer pressure?

## Further Practice 4 – Units 7 & 8

**5.** Read the text and find out what the numbers below correspond to.

### Facts and figures

It is our aim for the services we provide to assist survivors to become empowered, independent and resilient individuals. Numbers can misrepresent issues or be incredibly overwhelming, but they are important. Below you will find a fact sheet that gives an overview of the current facts and figures for slavery and trafficking in the UK and further afield.

1. Almost 21 million people worldwide are victims of forced labour — 11.4 million women and girls and 9.5 million men and boys.

2. Of those exploited by individuals or enterprises, 4.5 million are victims of forced sexual exploitation.

3. Forced labour in the private economy generates US $150 billion in illegal profits per year.

4. In the UK in 2015, 3,266 people were identified as potential victims of trafficking. This is a 40% increase on 2014 figures.

5. Of the 3,266 potential victims of trafficking identified in 2015, 982 of these were children.

6. There is no typical victim of slavery. Victims are men, women and children of all ages, ethnicities and nationalities and cut across the population. However, it's normally more prevalent among the most vulnerable or within minority or socially excluded groups. Approximately 53% of victims in the UK are women, and 46% are men. […]

7. Poverty, limited opportunities at home, lack of education, unstable social and political conditions, economic imbalances and war are some of the key drivers that contribute to someone's vulnerability in becoming a victim of modern slavery. […]

8. Potential victims have been reported from 103 different countries of origin in 2015. The top six most common countries of origin for potential victims of trafficking recorded in 2015 were Albania, Nigeria, Vietnam, Romania, Slovakia and the UK, with potential victims originating from Albania representing 18% of all referrals to the National Referral Mechanism last year. […]

Extracted from <www.unseenuk.org/about/the-problem/facts-and-figures>.
Accessed on May 19, 2016.

a. 21 million ♦
b. 4.5 million ♦
c. 34% ♦
d. 671 ♦
e. 61% ♦

**6.** Read the statements below and write T(True) or F (False).

   **a.** The organization Unseen tries to help victims of slavery overcome their terrible situation.

   **b.** Men and boys make up the majority of victims of slavery.

   **c.** The victims of sexual exploitation are exploited only by individuals.

   **d.** The number of potential victims of trafficking in the UK increased in 2014.

**7.** Identify the passages that correct the false statements that you have chosen in the previous activity and match them.

   **a.** "Almost 21 million people worldwide are victims of forced labour — 11.4 million women and girls and 9.5 million men and boys."

   **b.** "Of the 2,340 potential victims of trafficking identified in 2014, 671 of these were children."

   **c.** "The top six most common countries of origin for potential victims of trafficking recorded in 2014 were Albania, Nigeria, Vietnam, Romania, Slovakia and the UK […]"

   **d.** "Of those exploited by individuals or enterprises, 4.5 million are victims of forced sexual exploitation."

**8.** Answer the questions below and share your answers with the class.

   **a.** Where do most potential victims of trafficking come from?

   **b.** What are some of the main reasons that make some people so vulnerable to modern slavery?

   **c.** Compare what you have just read with Brazilian history: why did land owners in Brazil buy slaves during colonial times?

**9.** Read the quote below and, in pairs, discuss the question: do you agree with this point of view? Why?

> Child labor perpetuates poverty, unemployment, illiteracy, population growth, and other social problems.
> (Kailash Satyarthi, Indian child rights activist and Nobel Peace Prize winner)

Extracted from <www.brainyquote.com/quotes/keywords/child_labor.html>. Accessed on March 28, 2016.

# Further Practice 4 – Units 7 & 8

**10.** Work in pairs to write two sentences about forced labor and slavery around the world using the passive voice.

**11.** Read another excerpt of the summary report Violence Against Children in South Africa. Then answer the questions that follow.

## Violence against children
## IN THE COMMUNITY

Sometimes the communities or areas where children live are unsafe. Many children become victims of violence in places other than their homes or schools, such as the streets or parks they use. It was found that:

* 1 in every 5 cases of sexual assault took place in a residential street (in suburbs and townships).
* Boys are twice more likely to be murdered than girls (for every girl who is a victim of murder, two boys are victims of murder).
* Children younger than 5 years and children aged 15 to 17 years are most likely to be victims of murder.
* Children with disabilities are nearly twice more likely to become victims of violence, abuse or neglect than children who are not disabled.
* Children who are gay or lesbian are often victims of verbal abuse, teasing, violence and nasty comments.

There is also concern in some areas that children are involved in gangs and becoming victims of violence because often gangs are violent towards their own members, other children and even adults living in the community.

The study also identified some harmful and violent cultural practices involving children, especially where children are physically forced to do things. There were also incidents reported where children were killed for their body parts, which were used for witchcraft, *muti* or other purposes. The exact numbers of these incidents are unknown, but they do occur in some parts of the country.

These days many children have access to cellphones, Mxit or the Internet. These are very convenient ways to find information or stay in contact with friends. However, many children also become victims of cyberbullying. More than one third of children are victims of cyber-aggression.

**There are many reasons why children experience violence in their communities. Studies have shown that the availability of alcohol, drugs and weapons are often causes for violence against children.**

Extracted from <www.unicef.org/southafrica/SAF_resources_violenceagainstchildren.pdf>. Accessed on May 27, 2016.

a. Besides home, where else can children become victims of violence?

b. In your point of view, why are children with disabilities twice more likely to become victims of violence than the ones who are not disabled?

c. Read the passage below again and answer: why do children get involved in gangs?

> "There is also concern in some areas that children are involved in gangs and becoming victims of violence because often gangs are violent towards their own members, other children and even adults living in the community."

# EXAM PRACTICE

## Distracted Driving

Distracted driving consistently ranks as one of the traffic safety issues at forefront of many drivers' thinking. Each year, more than 80% of drivers in the annual AAA Foundation Traffic Safety Culture Index cite distraction as a serious problem and a behavior that makes them feel less safe on the road. Nearly half of all people who say they feel less safe than they did five years ago say distracted driving by other drivers fuels their concerns.

Distracted driving is a deadly behavior. Federal estimates suggest that distraction contributes to 16% of all fatal crashes, leading to around 5,000 deaths every year.

Extraído de: <www.aaafoundation.org/distracted-driving>. Acessado em: 6 de setembro de 2015.

Leia as proposições e assinale a alternativa correta.

I – A distração ao volante é fonte de grande preocupação para os motoristas, mas não chega a ser a maior delas.

II – A maioria dos motoristas reporta que a conduta ao volante dos demais é o fator que mais os preocupa.

III – A distração ao volante é a maior causa de acidentes com vítimas fatais.

IV – A distração ao volante é uma das causas dos acidentes com vítimas fatais, mas não é responsável pela maior parte deles.

a. V – V – F – V

b. F – V – F – V

c. F – F – F – V

d. V – V – F – F

e. F – V – F – F

# Career Planning

## Unit 1

### Journalist: job description

Journalists research, write, edit, proofread and file news stories, features and articles for use on television and radio or within magazines, journals and newspapers.

**What does a journalist do?** Typical employers | Qualifications and training | Key skills

Journalists write and assemble together news stories that will interest their audience. By gathering together a number of different sources and ensuring that all the arguments are represented, they keep their audience abreast of events in their world.

The job typically involves:

- reading press releases
- researching articles
- establishing and maintaining contacts
- interviewing sources
- writing, editing, and submitting copy

- attending events
- proofreading
- verifying statements and facts
- staying up-to-date with privacy, contempt and defamation law
- liaising with editors, sub-editors, designers and photographers.

Promotional prospects are good, with structured career paths and the possibility of transferring between television, radio, newspaper and publishing work.

**Typical employers of journalists**

- Newspapers
- Magazines
- Newswires
- Websites
- Radio stations
- Television companies
- Periodical publishers

Many journalists work freelance. However, to do so you will need a network of industry contacts, the ability to propose strong pitches and a reputation for reliability.

[…]

Extracted from <targetjobs.co.uk/careers-advice/job-descriptions/280509-journalist-job-description>. Accessed on September 7, 2015.

1. From your point of view, among all the journalists' tasks, which one is the most interesting? Why do you think so?

2. After reading this job description, would you like to be a journalist? Justify your answer.

# Unit 2

## What does a Political Scientist do?

A political scientist is an expert on the history, development, and applications of public policies and international relations. Professionals usually specialize in a particular field, such as conducting research and surveys on public opinion, advising politicians and important government officials, or providing commentary on policy decisions. A political scientist might work for a specific government office, private research institution, university, or a nonprofit awareness group.

Political science is an exciting, ever-changing field that is appealing to professionals with many different interests. Many people choose to become political scientists because they want to improve current social and economic conditions. They may work in government agencies or nonprofit organizations to develop statistics and advocate public awareness. Experts design and conduct surveys and research projects to analyze poverty rates, pollution levels, water and food quality, the condition of roads and public structures, and the effectiveness of government initiatives, among thousands of other variables. They use this information to write reports, educate officials and the public, and promote change.

A skilled political scientist may work for a specific politician or official, conducting research and providing expert advice on political decisions. He or she might specialize in certain types of policies, such as international affairs, Homeland Security, health care, education, or business development. Professionals help lawmakers determine the need for new approaches to public policies and suggest ways to achieve success.

Some experts in the field choose to become print or broadcast journalists, where they can offer facts and opinions to the public about current affairs and political decisions. Others become very involved in categorizing and analyzing historical political information. In addition, a knowledgeable political scientist might choose to teach college courses either full- or part-time. Some experts with strong credentials and public appeal even run for office themselves.

To become a political scientist, an individual is usually required to obtain at least a bachelor's degree in the field from an accredited college or university. Many professionals pursue advanced degrees to improve their knowledge, credentials, and job opportunities. [...]

Extracted from <www.wisegeek.com/what-does-a-political-scientist-do.htm>. Accessed on February 1, 2016.

**1.** What are the benefits of having political scientists working in your community?

**2.** If you were a political scientist, how would you improve the social and economic conditions of your community? Justify your answer.

# Career Planning

## Unit 3

## Historians Defined

**Question**
What does it take to be a historian and what do they do on a daily basis?

**Answer**
There are thousands of historians at work today, but they work in a wide variety of jobs and ways. Fundamentally, to be a historian you need to love digging into the raw materials of history and an enthusiasm for sharing what you find. But how and where someone works as a historian makes for a wide variety of stepping stones to a career.

To do history in a professional way generally requires an advanced degree in history or a closely related field. Historians who work at colleges and universities, for instance, typically need a doctoral degree to get a job.

[…]

Historians working as researchers (and this includes historians at colleges and universities as well as public historians) tend to do pretty similar types of work. They develop a sense of the standard opinions on a particular historical subject by reading what other historians have already written on the subject, and then they dig into the source materials to build a new interpretation or follow a new insight. These findings are then put together in any of a variety of forms, such as books, articles, websites, reports for clients, or museum scripts.

Historians working in academia tend to divide their time between their roles as researchers and their roles as teachers. As teachers they spend a significant amount of time preparing for classes, working with students, and assessing their students' work.

Historians working in other workplaces tend to divide their time as researchers with other types of activity – working as administrators at historical societies, for instance, or working with members of the general public at historic sites.

With more than 30,000 historians at work today, there are almost as many different opportunities to do history as there are ways of living the life of a historian from day-to-day.

Extracted from <teachinghistory.org/history-content/ask-a-historian/24120>. Accessed on September 7, 2015.

1. Do you think that historians can help us understand our present? Why/Why not?

2. If you were a historian, what area of research would you choose? Explain.

# Unit 4

## Music Composer: Career Info & Requirements

Music composers produce, arrange, and create music of all styles, from symphonies to rock to jingles. Read on to learn how to chase your dream of being a professional music composer.

### Career Definition for Music Composers

Music composers can do more than just create music for a large audience, as enviable as that sounds. Jobs are available conducting orchestras, composing soundtracks for films, writing songs for commercials, producing records, and teaching. […]

### Required Education

Many colleges and universities offer degrees such as a Bachelor of Arts in Music Composition, a Bachelor of Music in Music Composition, or a Bachelor of Science in Music Composition. Graduate degree possibilities include a Master of Arts in Music Composition, a Master of Music in Music Composition, and a Doctor of Philosophy in Music Composition. In most cases, an audition is required for students interested in pursuing these degrees; many schools also require students to perform their own compositions at a recital. Most bachelor's degree programs in music composition are rigorous and take four years or more to complete.

### Skills Required

Being a naturally talented musician is the first key to unlocking a career as a music composer. Proficiency with multiple instruments, singing abilities, and an appreciation of music history are all helpful attributes. Patience, persistence, and the ability to network and market one's talents are also needed in this daunting profession. […]

Extracted from <study.com/articles/Music_Composer_Career_Info_and_Requirements_for_Becoming_a_Professional_Composer.html>. Accessed on September 7, 2015.

1. Do you think that people are born with an appreciation for music and the ability to demonstrate it or do they develop musical ability through practice? Explain.

# Career Planning

## Unit 5

Promotes tourism and devises tourist development initiatives/campaigns with the aim of generating and increasing revenue.

### Tourism officer

### Job description

A tourism officer works to develop and enhance the visitor facilities of a region and to stimulate tourism growth in order to produce economic benefits for a particular region or site. They often work for local authorities but may also work within private companies or other public sector agencies.

### Work activities

- Promoting existing tourist attractions through advertising campaigns, developing promotional literature including artwork, writing press releases and copy for tourism guides/newsletters
- Carrying out research of existing tourist attractions to gain customer feedback in order to make improvements
- Researching local history and local people's views in order to develop potential new tourist attractions
- Working with the media and other local partner organisations to raise the profile of the local area, generate positive publicity and create a brand identity for the area
- Organising exhibition stands at conferences and holiday shows, both nationally and overseas, to promote the area
- Organising special and seasonal events and festivals
- Providing support, guidance and sometimes administering funding for local tourism-related business and advising new tourism businesses
- Encouraging the development of new jobs within the tourism sector
- Bringing in tourism development funding to the area
- Assessing the impact that any planned developments may have upon the local environment weighed against the potential benefits
- Consulting with local tourism businesses such as tour operators, restaurants and guest-houses, to assess the effectiveness of current tourism development policies and to develop an overall tourism development strategy.
[…]

### Entry requirements

Entry is possible without a third level qualification which means jobs are open to graduates from all disciplines, but relevant qualifications are becoming increasingly more in demand by employers. In addition, most employers ask for some previous experience within the travel and tourism industry. […]

Extracted from <gradireland.com/careers-advice/job-descriptions/tourism-officer>. Accessed on September 07, 2015.

1. Are there any activities that tourism officers do that you would like to try? Explain.

2. What could become a tourist attraction in your community? How would you promote it? Justify your answer.

# Unit 6

## Lawyers

### What Lawyers Do

Lawyers advise and represent individuals, businesses, and government agencies on legal issues and disputes.

### Duties of lawyers

Lawyers typically do the following:

- Advise and represent clients in courts, before government agencies, and in private legal matters
- Communicate with their clients, colleagues, judges and others involved in the case
- Conduct research and analysis of legal problems
- Interpret laws, rulings, and regulations for individuals and businesses
- Present facts in writing and verbally to their clients or others and argue on behalf of their clients
- Prepare and file legal documents, such as lawsuits, appeals, wills, contracts, and deeds

Lawyers, also called *attorneys*, act as both advocates and advisors.

As advocates, they represent one of the parties in criminal or civil trials by presenting evidence and arguing in support of their client.

As advisors, lawyers counsel their clients about their legal rights and obligations and suggest courses of action in business and personal matters. All attorneys research the intent of laws and judicial decisions and apply the laws to the specific circumstances that their clients face.

Lawyers often oversee the work of support staff, such as paralegals and legal assistants.

Lawyers may have different titles and different duties, depending on where they work.

[...]

### Lawyer Work Schedules

The majority of lawyers work full time, and many work more than the usual 40 hours per week. Lawyers who are in private practice or those who work in large firms often work additional hours, conducting research and preparing and reviewing documents.

### How to Become a Lawyer

All lawyers must have a law degree and must also typically pass a state's written bar examination. [...]

Extracted from <collegegrad.com/careers/lawyers>. Accessed on September 1, 2015.

**1.** Are there any aspects among lawyers' duties that attract you? Which ones? If not, why?

**2.** If you were a lawyer, what do you think you could do towards justice in your community?

# Career Planning

## Unit 7

### Nurse: job description

Nurses plan and provide medical and nursing care to patients in hospitals, at home or in other settings.

**What does a nurse do?**

Nurses work as part of a team of professional and medical staff that includes doctors, social workers and therapists.

Typical duties of the job include:
- assessing and planning nursing care requirements
- providing pre- and post-operation care
- monitoring and administering medication and intravenous infusions
- taking patient samples, pulses, temperatures and blood pressures
- writing records
- supervising junior staff
- organising workloads
- providing emotional support to patients and relatives
- tutoring student nurses

Twenty-four-hour shift work can be a requirement of the job.

**Typical employers of nurses**
- Hospitals
- NHS Trusts
- Residential homes
- Prisons
- Agencies
- Health centres
- Schools
- Companies
- GP practices
[...]

**Key skills for nurses**
- Good health and fitness
- Caring and compassionate nature
- Excellent teamwork and people skills
- Observational skills
- Ability to use initiative
- Ability to deal with emotionally charged and pressured situations
- Verbal and written communication skills
- Resilience
- Stamina

Adapted from <targetjobs.co.uk/careers-advice/job-descriptions/276221-nurse-job-description>.
Accessed on September 1, 2015.

**1.** Do you have any of the key skills needed to be a nurse? Which one(s)?

**2.** Would you like to be a nurse? Why (not)?

# Unit 8

## How to become a Sociologist

Most positions in the field of sociology require a very high degree of educational attainment, with a master's degree or a Ph.D. being required by most employers. The possession of a master's degree is usually enough to qualify for positions outside the educational sector, although there may be other requirements, depending on the field of specialization. Higher-level positions will almost always require a Ph.D. While a bachelor's degree is usually not enough to provide the employment opportunities available to sociologists with higher educational achievements, it can still be useful for a wide variety of entry-level jobs in related fields.

In most cases, an extensive background in statistics and mathematics is beneficial for many positions, particularly those that have to do with the different types of research methods. Since the nature of the job is always changing, sociologists would also benefit from computer skills as well as familiarity with the latest developments in their particular area of expertise.

### What does a Sociologist do?

The work of a sociologist involves studying different groups, cultures, organizations and social institutions. They are also often called upon to study the various social, religious, political, economic and business activities that people engage in. Sociologists are also often required to study how different groups of people react to such occurrences as the development of technology, health issues, criminal activity and various other social phenomena.

Sociologists employed in educational institutions often have to perform a number of tasks, including classroom instruction, researching, writing and even administrative roles.

### What skills or qualities do I need to become a Sociologist?

Most sociologists employed in corporate settings typically work regular hours. The job may entail working at a desk for long periods, either by themselves or with other sociologists. They will generally have to be prepared to read and prepare detailed reports and to deal with the pressures that are associated with writing articles on a deadline. You will also have to accept the fact that you may, from time to time, have to work overtime, without any monetary compensation. [...]

Extracted from <www.mypursuit.com/careers-19-3041.00/Sociologist.html>. Accessed on September 1, 2015.

1. Among the studies and tasks that sociologists carry out and perform, which ones would be useful in your community? Justify.

2. Would you like to be a sociologist? Why/Why not?

# Learning from Experience 1

## Our School Against Discrimination

### Objectives

- use experience as the primary foundation for learning;
- learn about different kinds of discrimination and promote effective individual and group interventions against prejudicial and discriminatory attitudes;
- organize and carry out a series of interviews with people from the school community who have been victims of some form of discriminatory attitude and publish them in a school print newspaper;
- reflect on the activity considering the process and the final results.

### Stage 1: Warming Up

Discuss the quote below with your classmates.

> "Prejudices are what fools use for reason."
> (Voltaire, French philosopher)

Extracted from <www.goodreads.com/quotes/88451-prejudices-are-what-fools-use-for-reason>. Accessed on September 7, 2015.

### Stage 2: Expanding Your Knowledge

Read the text below and find the two most significant pieces of information it conveys, in your opinion. Then compare your answers to your classmates'.

## Racism, Sexism and Homophobia

In daily life at school, teachers and school staff witness many interactions between various members of the school community. Some are characterized by unkindness, abuse, an intention to hurt or harm someone, or by a power imbalance, where one individual is afraid of or dominated by another.

Sometimes, social problems such as racism, sexism, homophobia, and other forms of injustice may take such direct and explicit forms. […]

When incidents, behaviour or practices involving racism, sexism and homophobia take place, there are other "actors" present, visible or not, in addition to the individuals who are directly involved. Some examples of "actors" that may influence a situation at school, even though they can't be seen or heard at the time are:

- television shows and movies;
- song lyrics;
- family culture;
- political decisions influencing school or family life;
- school books, newspapers, magazines and other literature;
- learned internal messages in someone's mind;
- billboards, posters and other forms of advertising.

This is because racism, sexism and homophobia are among a number of social problems that are embedded in our systems and institutions, in the way our society is organized. These forms of injustice are rooted in a historical legacy of social exclusion that continues to influence our society in ways that marginalize certain social groups. They are inextricably connected to everything teachers and other members of the school community (students, parents, administrators, support staff) say and do. They flow from and result in issues of Power and Identity. […]

Extracted from <www.safeatschool.ca/plm/equity-and-inclusion/racism-sexism-homophobia-social-problems>. Accessed on September 7, 2015.

## Stage 3: Getting Down to Action

- Work in groups of 8. Some of you will search for people from the school community who have been victims of some form of discriminatory behavior and invite them to be interviewed for the school newspaper; some will prepare and carry out interviews, while others will be in charge of the production and publication of the paper.
- Organize at least one meeting with the interviewees to explain their roles and your expectations for their contribution to the paper. Let them know that the more trustworthy they are while talking about their experiences as victims of prejudice and discrimination, the more they will be helping others not to be exposed to discriminatory behavior.
- Plan in advance how you will document the project preparation steps and the final product. Try to use different formats such as pictures, audio, and video recordings. This will be very useful while editing the final draft of the newspaper and in the evaluation process as well.
- While writing the paper, make sure to use language that is adequate to your target audience - students and the school community.
- Do not forget to create a logo for the newspaper.
- Have your teacher correct and comment all the writings before inserting them into the newspaper layout.
- Before the publication of the newspaper, make posters to promote it inside and outside the school.
- Print and deliver the newspaper inside and around the school. If possible, provide an online version of the publication as well.

## Stage 4: Analyzing and Sharing the Results

- Analyze the project's records. Prepare and carry out a class presentation, in English, on the procedures involved in the making of the newspaper. Each group is supposed to present information about the task they carried out. Use the pictures taken or the audio recordings made during the interviews; you might also use graphics or charts and their corresponding reports to present some interesting data collected during the interviews. Remember to have the final product (the newspaper itself) available for analysis as well.

## Stage 5: Reflecting and Evaluating

- Has the event engaged members of the community, school staff, and students in promoting awareness and promptness for a more thoughtful posture against discrimination?
- What have you learned from this experience? How can you improve the project so that it yields better results next time?

### EXTRA RESOURCES

- <revistaescola.abril.com.br/formacao/educacao-nao-tem-cor-425486.shtml>
- <www.ericdigests.org/pre-9215/racism.htm>
- <www.pbs.org/wnet/wideangle/lessons/brazil-in-black-and-white/discrimination-and-affirmative-action-in-brazil/?p=4323>
- <www.cidh.oas.org/countryrep/brazil-eng/Chaper%209%20.htm>
- <www.ipea.gov.br/portal/index.php?option=com_content&view=article&id=24533>

Accessed on September 7, 2015.

# Learning from Experience 2

## Literature Out Loud

### Objectives

- use experience as the primary foundation for learning;
- understand language as a means of expression and communication and enhance the taste for literary manifestations;
- read literary pieces from well-known authors and write your own about *friendship*;
- organize and conduct the event *Literature Out Loud: Friendship*;
- create an online invitation and posters to promote the event;
- reflect on the event considering the process and the results.

### Stage 1: Warming Up

Read the cartoon and, in pairs, discuss the importance of literature in your life. Then answer the questions that follow.

- How can bringing literature into our hearts, school, and home help us understand our deeper feelings such as love and friendship?
- What role does literature play in the development of language skills?

"It's called 'reading'. It's how people install new software into their brains"

### Stage 2: Expanding Your Knowledge

- Read the fable and discuss it with your classmates. What is the moral of the story?

## The Bear and the Two Travelers

[…]

Two men were traveling together, when a Bear suddenly met them on their path.

One of them climbed up quickly into a tree and concealed himself in the branches. The other, seeing that he would be attacked, fell flat on the ground. When the Bear came up and felt him with his snout, and smelt him all over, the Traveler held his breath, and pretended to be dead.

The Bear soon left the "dead" Traveler, for it is said a bear will not touch a dead body.

When the Bear was gone, the other Traveler descended from the tree, and asked his friend what it was the Bear had whispered in his ear.

"He gave me this advice," his companion replied. "Never travel with a friend who deserts you at the approach of danger."

[…]

Extracted from <www.aesop-fable.com/people/the-bear-and-the-two-travelers>. Accessed on September 8, 2015.

## Stage 3: Getting Down to Action

- Work in groups. Read and discuss the texts suggested by your teacher. Refer back to unit 4 and do some research on the subject matter *friendship* in order to compose your own literary piece. Remember to use language that is sensitive and fair to your target audience.

- After getting language feedback from your teacher, start making the arrangements for the event *Literature Out Loud: Friendship*. Remember to watch out for rhythm and intonation while reading your text aloud; rehearse as much as you can so as to improve your performance.

- Publish an online invitation for the event on the school website. You can also create posters to promote it and display them around the school. If possible, invite not only students from other classes and school staff members, but also your parents, friends, and people from the school community.

- Plan in advance to video record the event.

- Organize at least one rehearsal where all participants can be together.

## Stage 4: Analyzing and Sharing the Results

- Analyze the event's video recording. Prepare and carry out a class presentation, in English, on the contents of the event.

## Stage 5: Reflecting and Evaluating

- What have you learned from this experience? Has this project enhanced your taste for literary manifestations?
- How can you proceed the next time you engage in a similar task so as to improve the outcome?

### EXTRA RESOURCES

- <www.edutopia.org/poetry-slam-global-writes>
- <www.poetryinvoice.com/>

Accessed on September 8, 2015.

# Learning from Experience 3

## Festivals and Celebrations Around the World

FLIP 2014 – Festa Literária de Paraty.

### Objectives

- use experience as the primary foundation for learning;
- research about festivals and celebrations in Brazil and around the world;
- organize and conduct a class presentation using the software Prezi;
- analyze, present, and discuss the research findings;
- reflect on the task considering the process and the results.

### Stage 1: Warming Up

Read the quote below and decide whether or not you agree with it. Then share your opinion with the class.

> "Cultures, along with the religions that shape and nurture them, are value systems, sets of traditions and habits clustered around one or several languages, producing meaning: for the self, for the here and now, for the community, for life."
> (Tariq Ramadan, Swiss philosopher and writer)

Extracted from <www.brainyquote.com/quotes/quotes/t/tariqramad531538.html?src=t_traditions>. Accessed on September 8, 2015.

### Stage 2: Expanding Your Knowledge

Read the text and answer the question: When it comes to Brazilian traditions, festivals and celebrations, do you think that they bring culture closer to people? Why/Why not?

#### Legarda: Enrich Our Festivals, Preserve Our Culture

Press release
March 14, 2013

Reelectionist Senator Loren Legarda encouraged Filipinos to carry on with the tradition of celebrating festivals in towns and provinces during her visit to Pampanga.

Legarda, Chair of the Senate Committee on Cultural Communities, said that the conduct of grand and vibrant fiestas is part of the rich culture of the Philippines and it brings Filipino culture closer to the people.

"We must continue to enrich these celebrations, which not only remind us of the history and traditions of our towns and provinces, but also unite people and communities as they work together in making our festivals successful," she said.

The Senator explained that festivals are effective tools in preserving Philippine culture since these are conducted every year and involve everyone in the community including the young citizens.

She added that fiestas also help boost local economy through tourism, citing some major festivals in Pampanga, such as the Giant Lantern Festival, the Philippine International Hot Air Balloon Fiesta, the Piestang Tugak or Frog Festival, the Apung Iru Fluvial Festival, and the Sinukwan Festival.

"Since Filipinos enjoy these fiestas in their towns and provinces, these celebrations become effective channels in bringing our culture closer to the people, especially to the youth," she stressed.

"I urge all Filipinos to take that extra step of knowing more about the story behind the festivals in our country and take to heart the traditions passed on by our forefathers as these cultural treasures constitute the Filipino soul," Legarda concluded.

Extracted from <www.senate.gov.ph/press_release/2013/0314_legarda2.asp>. Accessed on September 8, 2015.

## Stage 3: Getting Down to Action

- Work in small groups. Research about festivals and celebrations in Brazil and around the world. Focus on different cultural aspects, traditions and feasts.
- Don't forget to document your research. Remember to gather not only pieces of written information, but also photos that illustrate what is being talked about.
- Gather all the data the group has found and bring it to the classroom.
- After listing the most interesting pieces of information collected, discuss them within your group, and choose one tradition or festivity to prepare your presentation using Prezi or another presentation software. Don't forget to use language that is adequate to your target audience.

## Stage 4: Analyzing and Sharing the Results

- After the presentations, discuss whether those traditions and celebrations help keep the corresponding culture alive or are just used as a means to enhance tourism.
- Consider sharing the presentation document on the school website. You can also make posters and hang them inside the school, where the school community can have access to the research findings.

## Stage 5: Reflecting and Evaluating

- How does this research help students and the school community? Does it contribute to discovering, valuing, and respecting other peoples' traditions, festivals and celebrations?
- What have you learned from this experience? How can you expand this type of research to effectively promote knowledge and reflection about different cultures?

### EXTRA RESOURCES

- <super.abril.com.br/10-festivais-curiosos-ao-redor-do-mundo>
- <www.visitmexico.com/pt/tradicoes-e-festas-religiosas-do-mexico>
- <www.factmonster.com/ipka/A0909585.html>
- <prezi.com/signup/public/>
- <prezi.com/explore/staff-picks/>

Accessed on September 9, 2015.

# Learning from Experience 4

## Anti-Alcohol Awareness Campaign

### Objectives
- use experience as the primary foundation for learning;
- learn about the harms caused by alcohol consumption and its effects at school, in the family, in the community, and in our society as a whole;
- show the negative impacts of alcohol abuse through an anti-alcohol awareness campaign;
- create campaign posters and videos to promote awareness;
- reflect on the campaign considering the process and the results.

### Stage 1: Warming Up
Take a look at the campaign poster and, in pairs, discuss the consequences of alcohol consumption in people's lives.

### Stage 2: Expanding Your Knowledge
Work in pairs. Read a passage from an article about alcohol and teens. Then talk about how it relates to your discussion in Stage 1. Finally, report your conclusions to the class.

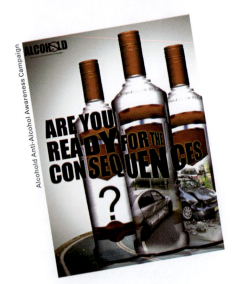

## Alcohol and Teens

[…]

**What are the dangerous effects of alcohol use in teens?**

Just a few of the many dangers of alcohol use in teens include the following:
- Alcohol decreases teens' ability to pay attention.
- Teens who have experienced alcohol withdrawal tend to have difficulties with memory.
- The teenage brain that has been exposed to alcohol is at risk for being smaller in certain parts.

[…]

- Male teens who drink heavily tend to complete fewer years of education compared to male teens who do not.
- The younger a person is when they begin drinking, the more likely they are to develop a problem with alcohol.
- Each year, almost 2,000 people under the age of 21 die in car crashes in which underage drinking is involved. Alcohol is involved in nearly half of all violent deaths involving youth.
- In 2010, 56% of drivers 15 to 20 years of age who were killed in motor-vehicle crashes after drinking and driving were not wearing a seat belt.
- More than three times the number of eighth-grade girls who drink heavily said they have attempted suicide compared to girls in that grade who do not drink.
- Intoxication is associated with suicide attempts using more lethal methods, and positive blood alcohol levels are often found in people who complete suicide.

- Teens who drink are more likely to engage in sexual activity, have unprotected sex, have sex with a stranger, or be the victim or perpetrator of a sexual assault.
- Excess alcohol use can cause or mask other emotional problems, like anxiety or depression.
- Drinking in excess can lead to the use of other drugs, like marijuana, cocaine, or heroin.

[...]

Extracted from <www.medicinenet.com/alcohol_and_teens/article.htm#what_are_the_dangerous_effects_of_alcohol_use_in_teens>. Accessed on September 9, 2015.

## Stage 3: Getting Down to Action

- Work in small groups.
- Research about the harms caused by alcohol consumption and its effects at school, in the family, in the community, and in our society as a whole.
- Decide on which danger or effect of alcohol consumption you want to focus and start planning your campaign poster and video. Do not forget to take your target audience into account.
- Show your poster and video campaign to your teacher and make the necessary adjustments after correction.
- Promote the campaign inside the school.

## Stage 4: Analyzing and Sharing the Results

- Talk to people inside the school about the posters and videos of the campaign. Observe their reactions to evaluate if they responded to your message as you had expected them to.
- Carry out a class discussion on how you addressed the target audience to convince them to take action and contribute to a reduction in harm linked to alcohol consumption, especially among the youth.
- Present your conclusions on the effectiveness of your campaign.

## Stage 5: Reflecting and Evaluating

- How were the people involved in the campaign inspired by your cause? Have your campaign poster and video provoked a call for action? Explain your answers.
- What else can you do to encourage people, especially the younger generation, to keep away from the dangers of alcohol?

### EXTRA RESOURCES

- <www.drinkingnightmare.gov.au/internet/drinkingnightmare/publishing.nsf/content/about-the-campaign>
- <apps.einstein.br/alcooledrogas/novosite/orientacoes_escola.htm>
- <www.antidrogas.com.br/mostraartigo.php?c=814&msg=%B4A%20depend%EAncia%20de%20drogas%20%E9%20a%20doen%E7a%20mais%20democr%E1tica%20que%20existe,%20atinge%20todas%20as%20classes%20sociais%B4>
- <www.youtube.com/user/alcoholthinkagain>

Accessed on September 9, 2015.

# Studying for Enem

Enem 2010

Disponível em: http://www.meganbergdesigns.com/andrill/iceberg07/postcards/index.html. Acesso em: 29 jul. 2010 (adaptado).

Os cartões-postais costumam ser utilizados por viajantes que desejam enviar notícias dos lugares que visitam a parentes e amigos. Publicado no *site* do projeto ANDRILL, o texto em formato de cartão-postal tem o propósito de

**a.** comunicar o endereço da nova sede do projeto nos Estados Unidos.

**b.** convidar colecionadores de cartões-postais a se reunirem em um evento.

**c.** anunciar uma nova coleção de selos para angariar fundos para a Antártica.

**d.** divulgar às pessoas a possibilidade de receberem um cartão-postal da Antártica.

**e.** solicitar que as pessoas visitem o *site* do mencionado projeto com maior frequência.

Enem 2011

A tira, definida como um segmento de história em quadrinhos, pode transmitir uma mensagem com efeito de humor. A presença desse efeito no diálogo entre John e Garfield acontece porque

**a.** John pensa que sua ex-namorada é maluca e que Garfield não sabia disso.

**b.** Jodell é a única namorada maluca que John teve, e Garfield acha isso estranho.

**c.** Garfield tem certeza de que a ex-namorada de John é sensata, o maluco é o amigo.

**d.** Garfield conhece as ex-namoradas de John e considera mais de uma como maluca.

**e.** John caracteriza a ex-namorada como maluca e não entende a cara de Garfield.

Enem 2012

**I, too**

I, too, sing America.
I am the darker brother.
They send me to eat in the kitchen
When company comes,
But I laugh,
And eat well,
And grow strong.

Tomorrow,
I'll be at the table
When company comes.
Nobody'll dare
Say to me,
"Eat in the kitchen,"
Then.

Besides,
They'll see how beautiful I am
And be ashamed —

I, too, am America.

HUGHES, L. In: RAMPERSAD, A.; ROESSEL, D. (Ed.) The collected poems of Langston Hughes. New York: Knopf, 1994.

Langston Hughes foi um poeta negro americano que viveu no século XX e escreveu *I, too* em 1932. No poema, a personagem descreve uma prática racista que provoca nela um sentimento de

a. coragem, pela superação.
b. vergonha, pelo retraimento.
c. compreensão, pela aceitação.
d. superioridade, pela arrogância.
e. resignação, pela submissão.

23 February 2012 Last update at 16:53 GMT
BBC World Service
**J. K. Rowling to pen first novel for adults**

Author J. K. Rowling has announced plans to publish her first novel for adults, which will be "very different" from the Harry Potter books she is famous for. The book will be published worldwide although no date or title has yet been released. "The freedom to explore new territory is a gift that Harry's sucess has brought me", Rowling said.

All the Potter books were published by Bloomsbury, but Rowling has chosen a new publisher for her debut into adult fiction. "Although I've enjoyed writing it every bit as much, my next book will be very different to the Harry Potter series, which has been published so brilliantly by Bloomsbury and my other publishers around the world", she said, in a statement. "I'm delighted to have a second publishing home in Little, Brown, and a publishing team that will be a great partner in this new phase of my writing life".

Disponível em: www.bbc.co.uk. Acesso em: 24 fev. 2012 (adaptado).

J. K. Rowling tornou-se famosa por seus livros sobre o bruxo Harry Potter e suas aventuras, adaptados para o cinema. Esse texto, que aborda a trajetória da escritora britânica, tem por objetivo

# Studying for Enem

a. informar que a famosa série *Harry Potter* será adaptada para o público adulto.

b. divulgar a publicação do romance por J. K. Rowling inteiramente para adultos.

c. promover a nova editora que irá publicar os próximos livros de J. K. Rowling.

d. informar que a autora de *Harry Potter* agora pretende escrever para adultos.

e. anunciar um novo livro da série *Harry Potter* publicado por editora diferente.

Enem 2013

### Do one thing for diversity and inclusion

The United Nations Alliance of Civilizations (UNAOC) is launching a campaign aimed at engaging people around the world to *Do One Thing* to support Cultural Diversity and Inclusion. Every one of us can do ONE thing for diversity and inclusion; even one very little thing can become a global action if we all take part in it.

**Simple things YOU can do to celebrate the World Day for Cultural Diversity for Dialogue and Development on May 21.**

1. Visit an art exhibit or a museum dedicated to other cultures.
2. Read about the great thinkers of other cultures.
3. Visit a place of worship different than yours and participate in the celebration.
4. Spread your own culture around the world and learn about other cultures.
5. Explore music of a different culture.

There are thousands of things that you can do, **are you taking part in it?**

UNITED NATIONS ALLIANCE OF CIVILIZATIONS. Disponível em: www.unaoc.org. Acesso em: 16 fev. 2013 (adaptado).

Internautas costumam manifestar suas opiniões sobre artigos on-line por meio da postagem de comentários. O comentário que exemplifica o engajamento proposto na quarta dica da campanha apresentada no texto é

a. "Lá na minha escola, aprendi a jogar capoeira para uma apresentação no Dia da Consciência Negra."

b. "Outro dia assisti na TV uma reportagem sobre respeito à diversidade. Gente de todos os tipos, várias tribos. Curti bastante."

c. "Eu me inscrevi no Programa Jovens Embaixadores para mostrar o que tem de bom em meu país e conhecer outras formas de ser."

d. "Curto muito bater papo na internet. Meus amigos estrangeiros me ajudam a aperfeiçoar minha proficiência em língua estrangeira."

e. "Pesquisei em *sites* de culinária e preparei uma festa árabe para uns amigos da escola. Eles adoraram, principalmente, os doces!"

Disponível em: www.gocomics.com. Acesso em: 26 fev. 2012.

A partir da leitura dessa tirinha, infere-se que o discurso de Calvin teve um efeito diferente do pretendido, uma vez que ele

a. decide tirar a neve do quintal para convencer seu pai sobre seu discurso.

b. culpa o pai por exercer influência negativa na formação de sua personalidade.

c. comenta que suas discussões com o pai não correspondem às suas expectativas.

d. conclui que os acontecimentos ruins não fazem falta para a sociedade.

e. reclama que é vítima de valores que o levam a atitudes inadequadas.

Enem 2014

> **The Road Not Taken (by Robert Frost)**
>
> Two roads diverged in a wood, and I –
>
> I took the one less traveled by,
>
> And that has made all the difference.

Disponível em: www.poetryfoundation.org.
Acesso em: 29 nov. 2011 (fragmento).

Estes são os versos finais do famoso poema *The Road Not Taken*, do poeta americano Robert Frost. Levando-se em consideração que a vida é comumente metaforizada como uma viagem, esses versos indicam que o autor

a. festeja o fato de ter sido ousado na escolha que fez em sua vida.

b. lamenta por ter sido um viajante que encontrou muitas bifurcações.

c. viaja muito pouco e que essa escolha fez toda a diferença em sua vida.

d. reconhece que as dificuldades em sua vida foram todas superadas.

e. percorre várias estradas durante as diferentes fases de sua vida.

# Language Reference

## Unit 1

### Subject and Object Pronouns

Usamos *subject pronouns* para evitar a repetição dos sujeitos nas orações. Em português, os *subject pronouns* correspondem aos pronomes pessoais do caso reto.

*Patricia needs help with her English lessons. That's why Patricia is taking private lessons with Ms. Miller.*

*Patricia needs help with her English lessons. That's why **she**'s taking private lessons with Ms. Miller.*

*Our parents can't afford a new house at the beach right now. On the contrary, our parents are cutting down on their expenses.*

*Our parents can't afford a new house at the beach right now. On the contrary, **they** are cutting down on their expenses.*

Usamos *object pronouns* para substituir os objetos das orações. Em português, eles correspondem aos pronomes pessoais do caso oblíquo.

*My grandparents don't visit **us** very often. But they sure call **me** every other day.*

*Did you talk to your friends about the party or did you decide to keep **them** in the dark this time?*

Observe a tabela abaixo.

|  | Subject Pronouns | Object Pronouns |
|---|---|---|
| Singular | I | me |
| | you | you |
| | he | him |
| | she | her |
| | it | it |
| Plural | we | us |
| | you | you |
| | they | them |

**1.** Read the text below and identify the pronouns. Write S for the ones that are used as Subjects and O for the ones that are used as Objects.

@Work Advice: Fighting salary discrimination
By Karla L. Miller October 11, 2012

**Reader**: My company has a policy that, after so many years, your salary should be at mid-level on its salary charts. I'm now past that point. I've earned excellent reviews, have strong knowledge in my field and am continuing my education. I have brought this policy up during my appraisal, only to be told I am not eligible for a raise beyond that allotted, with no explanations. Recently it came to light that out of all of us who do this job, only the male worker in the group (with the same amount of time in the company as I have but less education) makes the mid-level salary rate. Appraisals are coming around again. Do I ask for another increase to bring my salary in line with the company policy? Or is it time to pursue another course of action?

**Karla**: Last week, we discussed how to ask for a raise without dragging higher-paid co-workers into the discussion. However, your situation as described has a whiff of gender bias about it. Some dragging may be in order.

But before you cry "Title VII!" and let slip the dogs of law, employment attorney Sharon Snyder of Ober | Kaler recommends giving your employer a chance to "do the right thing, for the right reason".

Snyder notes that your company's policy of tying salary to time served probably lacks the force of law. But it's a good place to start. If you're told again that you're "not eligible," press for explicit reasons why the policy doesn't apply to you.

If that tack gets you nowhere, start plugging your stellar record and value to the company, including your additional education and training.

No soap? Time to reveal what you know about your male co-worker's pay. Spell out how the disparity in your salaries inaccurately reflects your respective qualifications and contributions, and that you should be making at least as much as your co-worker, given your equal time served.

But, Snyder warns, don't mention discrimination yet. Just see what the boss says. If you get the raise, well done. If you're told there isn't enough money, ask for a timeline of when you can expect more; maybe you can get a raise in increments over the year. If you're told your performance falls short, discuss ways to improve it.

Extracted from <www.washingtonpost.com/lifestyle/magazine/atwork-advice-fighting-salary-discrimination/2012/10/05/bf263010-035c-11e2-8102-ebee9c66e190_story.html>. Accessed on August 7, 2015.

**2.** What do the pronouns in italics refer to? Explain. The first one is done for you.

**a.** "However, your situation as described has a whiff of gender bias about *it*."

It *refers to the situation of salary discrimination the woman is facing.*

**b.** "If you're told again that you're "not eligible", press for explicit reasons why the policy doesn't apply to *you*."

**c.** "If that tack gets *you* nowhere, start plugging your stellar record and value to the company, including your additional education and training."

**d.** "If you're told your performance falls short, discuss ways to improve *it*."

## Compounds with Some, Any and No

*Some* e *any* podem desempenhar a função de adjetivo, quando acompanham substantivos, ou de pronome, quando substituem um substantivo. *No* desempenha a função de adjetivo, e *none* de pronome. *Some, any, no* e seus respectivos derivados são usados quando nos referirmos a pessoas, lugares ou coisas que não conhecemos ou não sabemos especificar com precisão.

Leia os exemplos abaixo.

The students have **some** doubts about the end-of-the year schedule. **Some** sent me a few questions through the school website.

A: Have you got **any** ideas on what I can buy for Anna's birthday?
B: Sorry. I haven't got **any**.

A: I have **no** classes today. What about you?
B: Well, I have **none** either.

Observe que *some* é usado em frases afirmativas, ofertas, pedidos ou em perguntas, quando esperamos uma resposta positiva. *Any* é usado em frases negativas e interrogativas, e *no* e *none* são empregados em frases afirmativas, conferindo a elas sentido negativo.

Os compostos terminados em -*body* (ou -*one*) e -*thing* referem-se a pessoas e coisas, respectivamente, e seguem as mesmas regras de emprego de *some*, *any* e *no*.

# Language Reference

Leia:

A: *Is there **anybody** in your house today?*

B: *Yeah. There must be **somebody** there. Why?*

A: ***Nothing** special. I just need to drop by and hand in **something** I bought for your brother.*

**1.** Choose the correct words in the quotations below.

**a.** "There should be **any / no** discrimination against languages people speak, skin color, or religion." (Malala Yousafzai, Pakistani Activist)

<small>Extracted from <www.brainyquote.com/quotes/quotes/m/malalayous662527.html>. Accessed on August 8, 2015.</small>

**b.** "I resolutely believe that respect for diversity is a fundamental pillar in the eradication of racism, xenophobia and intolerance. There is **no / any** excuse for evading the responsibility of finding the most suitable path toward the elimination of **any / some** expression of discrimination against indigenous peoples." (Rigoberta Menchu, Guatemalan Indigenous Rights Activist)

<small>Extracted from <www.betterworld.net/quotes/endracism-quotes.htm>. Accessed on August 8, 2015.</small>

**2.** Complete the quotations below with the words from the box. Write the answers in your notebook.

| anyone | nobody | nothing | someone | something |
|--------|--------|---------|---------|-----------|

**a.** "♦ can hurt me without my permission". (Mahatma Gandhi, Indian leader)

<small>Extracted from <www.brainyquote.com/quotes/quotes/m/mahatmagan109079.html>. Accessed on August 8, 2015.</small>

**b.** "Happiness is not ♦ ready-made. It comes from your own actions". (Dalai Lama, Tibetan Leader)

<small>Adapted from <www.brainyquote.com/quotes/quotes/d/dalailama166116.html>. Accessed on August 8, 2015.</small>

**c.** "A wise woman wishes to be no one's enemy; a wise woman refuses to be ♦'s victim". (Maya Angelou, American Poet)

<small>Extracted from <www.brainyquote.com/quotes/quotes/m/mayaangelo578805.html>. Accessed on August 8, 2015.</small>

**d.** "There is ♦ I fear more than waking up without a program that will help me bring a little happiness to those with no resources, those who are poor, illiterate, and ridden with terminal disease". (Nelson Mandela, South African Statesman)

<small>Extracted from <www.brainyquote.com/quotes/quotes/n/nelsonmand447238.html>. Accessed on August 8, 2015.</small>

**e.** "The worst moment in my life was when I was seven years old and I discovered that there was a thing such as racism. You don't know you're different until ♦ lets you know. (Sanjeev Bhaskar, British Comedian)

<small>Extracted from <www.brainyquote.com/quotes/quotes/s/sanjeevbha618230.html?src=t_racism>. Accessed on August 8, 2015.</small>

# Unit 2

## Discourse Markers

Usamos *discourse markers* para estabelecer relações lógicas entre ideias, organizar e controlar o que dizemos ou escrevemos.

No quadro abaixo, observe alguns *discourse markers* comuns em inglês e as ideias que eles expressam.

| Marcadores do discurso | Expressam ideias de |
|---|---|
| And; also; besides; moreover; in addition | adição |
| Or; nor; whether; either; neither | alternativa |
| As; because; due to; since | causa |
| As; like | comparação |
| Although; even though; in spite of | concessão |
| As long as; except if; if; if not; unless | condição |
| Yet; but; however; on the other hand; conversely | contraste |
| For instance; for example; particularly; such as | exemplificação |
| To; in order to; so as to | propósito |
| First; second; next; after that; then; previously; finally | sequência |

Atente para os exemplos a seguir.

*I don't have enough money to travel abroad this year.* **Besides**, *I'll take a summer course in January* **and** *I have to stick around.*

**Either** *Jarrod* **or** *Ken will call.* **Although** *they're not interested in the job opening, I'm sure one of them will get in touch to thank us for the opportunity.*

**Since** *my parents will be out of town this weekend, I'm sure I'll have to work* **like** *a slave to keep everything in order.*

**In spite of** *the heavy rain, Ted and Karen decided to travel to the country house.* **As long as** *the family is together, it doesn't matter where they are: that's their motto.*

*We told Chris the truth about her brother.* **However**, *she may not believe us.*

*Why don't you take up a hobby* **such as** *gardening or painting?*

**In order to** *promote a clearer understanding of my research findings, I'm going to start my presentation talking about its main objectives.*

**First** *wash the fruits.* **Then** *peel and chop all of them.*

**1.** Read the text, pay attention to the discourse markers in bold, and match the columns according to the meanings they convey.

### Empowering women
[…]
### Key issues

Experience has shown that addressing gender equality and women's empowerment requires strategic interventions at all levels of programming and policy-making. Key issues include:

*Reproductive health*: The ability of women to control their own fertility is fundamental to women's empowerment and equality. When a woman can plan her family, she can plan the rest of her life. Protecting and promoting her reproductive rights – including the right to decide the number, timing and spacing of her children – is essential to ensuring her freedom to participate more fully and equally in society.

Language Reference 169

# Language Reference

> **In addition**, for both physiological and social reasons, women are more vulnerable than men to reproductive health problems. Collectively, complications of pregnancy or childbirth are the number two killer of women of reproductive age. Failure to provide information, services and conditions to help women protect their reproductive health constitutes gender-based discrimination and is a violation of women's rights to health and life.
>
> *Economic empowerment*: Six out of 10 of the world's poorest people are women. Economic disparities persist partly **because** much of the unpaid work within families and communities falls on the shoulders of women, and because women continue to face discrimination in the economic sphere.
>
> *Educational empowerment*: About two thirds of the world's illiterate adults are women. Lack of an education severely restricts a woman's access to information and opportunities. **Conversely**, increasing women's and girls' educational attainment benefits both individuals and future generations. Higher levels of women's education are strongly associated with lower infant mortality and lower fertility, **as well as** better outcomes for their children.
>
> *Political empowerment*: Gender equality cannot be achieved without the backing and enforcement of institutions. **But** too many social and legal institutions still do not guarantee women equality in basic legal and human rights, in access to or control of resources, in employment or earnings, **or** in social or political participation. **And** men continue to occupy most positions of political and legal authority; globally, only 22 per cent of parliamentarians are women. Laws against domestic violence are often not enforced on behalf of women.
>
> Last updated 3 March 2015.

Extracted from <www.unfpa.org/gender-equality>. Accessed on September 10, 2015.

**a.** as well as, and, in addition,   ♦ contrast

**b.** but, conversely   ♦ cause

**c.** because   ♦ alternative

**d.** or   ♦ addition

**2.** Choose the correct alternative to complete the text below.

> [...]
>
> ### Charting a new path for women in medicine and healthcare
>
> A true pioneer in the field of medicine, throughout her childhood she attended all boys' schools to study science. **Dr. Josephine Namboze** is East and Central Africa's first female medical doctor, ♦ the first woman in Africa to head an institute of public health. ♦ the first ever Representative for the World Health Organization in Botswana, she also wrote extensively about how race is not a determining factor in infectious and non-infectious disease. ♦ the first woman professor of medicine in East Africa, she didn't just break the glass ceiling, ♦ shattered it becoming a role model for many.
> [...]

Extracted from <beijing20.unwomen.org/en/voices-and-profiles/women-of-achievement>. Accessed on September 10, 2015.

**a.** besides / except if / also / however

**b.** finally / as / either / moreover

**c.** and / because / also / yet

**d.** and / as / also / but

# Unit 3

## Relative Pronouns

Os *relative pronouns* são usados quando queremos acrescentar informações sobre uma pessoa, coisa, lugar etc. mencionado anteriormente. As orações introduzidas pelos pronomes relativos são chamadas *relative clauses*.

Utilizamos o pronome relativo *who* para nos referirmos a pessoas. *Which* é empregado quando o antecedente não é uma pessoa, ou seja, para coisas, animais e ideias. *That* substitui *who* e *which* na maioria dos casos, mas é mais informal do que ambos.

Leia as seguintes frases.

*The man **who / that** entered the office a minute ago is asking for information.*

*The photo **which / that** you took at Carl's birthday party is fantastic!*

O pronome relativo *where* é usado para lugares e *when* para referências de tempo. Observe.

*The street **where** I live is extremely noisy at any time of the day.*

*Christmas is **when** people tend to get more emotional.*

O pronome relativo *whose* é usado para indicar posse e antecede um substantivo.

*The mother **whose** son is sick is waiting outside to talk to the principal.*

## Prepositions of Time (in, on, at)

As preposições *in, on* e *at* podem ser usadas para expressar a ideia de tempo.

*In* é usado antes de períodos do dia, meses, anos, décadas, séculos e estações do ano.

Leia os exemplos abaixo.

*I prefer to practice physical exercises **in** the morning.*

*Shop windows often look lovely **in** December.*

*Do trees grow new leaves **in** the spring or **in** the fall?*

*The twins weren't born **in** 2000. They were born **in** 1999.*

*Mini-skirts were trendy **in** the 1960's.*

*On* é usado antes de períodos específicos do dia, dias da semana, dias do mês e datas completas.

*Class 202 has Art lessons **on** Monday afternoons.*

*Our parents don't allow us to go out at night **on** Mondays or any other weekdays.*

*Daniel's prom will take place **on** April 3rd, 2020.*

*At* é usado antes de horas, palavras específicas para certos períodos do dia, datas e celebrações que não tenham a palavra *day*.

*What were you doing **at** a quarter past nine yesterday?*

*Meet me in front of the restaurant **at** noon, will you?*

*We're going to visit our relatives in Minas Gerais **at** Easter.*

*Driving downtown is not safe **at** night.*

# Language Reference

**1.** Complete the text with relative pronouns.

### Nixiwaka and the Yawanawá tribe (Brazil)
[...]
### Our culture
Our education begins at birth. We are taught to fish, hunt, gather fruits and plant our gardens.

We also have schools in our villages ♦ we can practice our Yawanawá language and remember our traditional stories and legends. We also learn Portuguese and use technology like mobile phones and computers so we can communicate with outsiders. We even use Facebook!

We have two shamans or spiritual leaders in our tribe: 'Yawa' and 'Tata'. They are more than one hundred years old! If one of them were to pass on without teaching their knowledge, information about our language, culture, the rainforest and its healing plant medicines would be lost forever. For this reason we have started to write down the names of different plants used for medicines and recording our rituals and ceremonies.

The Yawanawá people are known for their songs and their stories. Our songs are old and reflect our lives within nature. My favourite song is called 'wakomaya', ♦ means happiness – a song we sing to welcome visitors and to ♦ we dance to whilst holding hands.
[...]

Adapted from <www.survivalinternational.org/nixiwaka>. Accessed on September 10, 2015.

**2.** Read the excerpts below and pick out the correct prepositions to complete them.

a.
### Wave of attacks hits Brazil's Guarani tribe
10 September 2015
[...]
Gunmen have launched a wave of attacks against Guarani Indians in central Brazil.

*At / In / On* 29 August Guarani leader Semião Vilhalva was shot dead one week after his community reoccupied part of their ancestral land. A one-year-old baby was struck in the head by a rubber bullet, and many others were injured.

Less than a week later, *at / in / on* 3 September, 30 vehicles full of ranchers and gunmen arrived at the community of Guyra Kambi'y.
[...]

Extracted from <www.survivalinternational.org/news/10904>. Accessed on September 10, 2015.

b.
### Exposed: Forced evictions in Ethiopia – what the UK government tried to cover up
3 September 2015
[...]
The U.K. government tried to suppress evidence of gross human rights abuses in Ethiopia to appease the government there, a new investigation by Survival International, the global movement for tribal peoples' rights, has revealed.

The key aid donors to Ethiopia, including the U.K.'s DFID, USAID and the European Union, sent two missions to the Lower Omo Valley in the south of the country *at / in / on* August 2014, to investigate whether tribes there were being forced off their land to make way for commercial plantations.
[...]

Extracted from <www.survivalinternational.org/news/10894>. Accessed on September 10, 2015.

# Unit 4

## Present Perfect I

O *Present Perfect* é geralmente usado para descrever ações que aconteceram em um momento não determinado do passado. Tais ações podem ou não ter consequências no presente. Quando mencionamos ou sugerimos o tempo exato em que as ações ocorreram, usamos o *Simple Past*.

Para formarmos o *Present Perfect* usamos: verbo *has / have* + particípio passado do verbo principal.

Leia os exemplos a seguir.

*I* **have ('ve) bought** *a new PC tablet.*

*Jake* **has ('s) been** *to Rio.*

Na forma negativa, inserimos *not* depois de *have / has* e antes do verbo principal.

Veja.

*I* **have not (haven't) bought** *a new PC tablet.*

*Jake* **has not (hasn't) been** *to Rio.*

Na forma interrogativa, invertemos a posição de *have / has* com os sujeitos.

Observe.

**Have** *I* **bought** *a new PC tablet?*

**Has** *Jake* **been** *to Rio?*

O particípio passado dos verbos regulares tem a mesma forma usada no *Simple Past* (terminada em *-ed*).

Os verbos irregulares não seguem uma regra específica. A lista completa dos verbos irregulares usados neste volume está na página 189.

Observe mais exemplos na tabela abaixo.

| Affirmative | Negative | Interrogative |
| --- | --- | --- |
| I **have** / I**'ve left** the car keys at home. | I **have not** / I **haven't left** the car keys at home. | **Have** I **left** the car keys at home? |
| You **have** / You**'ve done** the dishes. | You **have not** / You **haven't done** the dishes. | **Have** you **done** the dishes? |
| He **has** / He**'s lived** abroad. | He **has not** / He **hasn't lived** abroad. | **Has** he **lived** abroad? |
| She **has** / She**'s prepared** the drinks for the party. | She **has not** / She **hasn't prepared** the drinks for the party. | **Has** she **prepared** the drinks for the party? |
| It **has** / It**'s been extremely** cold. | It **has not** / It **hasn't** been extremely cold. | **Has** it **been** extremely cold? |
| We **have** / We**'ve traveled** to the country. | We **have not** / We **haven't traveled** to the country. | **Have** we **traveled** to the country? |
| You **have** / You**'ve cooked** dinner. | You **have not** / You **haven't cooked** dinner. | **Have** you **cooked** dinner? |
| They **have** / They**'ve left** the office. | They **have not** / They **haven't left** the office. | **Have** they **left** the office? |

# Language Reference

## Short Answers – Affirmative and Negative

Para formarmos as respostas curtas (*short answers*) no *Present Perfect*, usamos *have / has* para respostas afirmativas e *haven't / hasn't* para respostas negativas.

|  | Short answers | |
|---|---|---|
|  | **Affirmative** | **Negative** |
| Has she gotten married? | Yes, she **has**. | No, she **hasn't**. |
| Have you seen Andrew around? | Yes, I **have**. | No, I **haven't**. |

**1.** Use the prompts from the box to complete the quotes below in the present perfect tense.

| everybody else / come | failure / be | friendship / belong | you / not learn |
|---|---|---|---|

a. "Friendship is the hardest thing in the world to explain. It's not something you learn in school. But if ♦ the meaning of friendship, you really haven't learned anything." (Muhammad Ali, American boxer and activist)

<sub>Extracted from <thinkexist.com/quotation/friendship-is_not_something_you_learn_in_school/214744.html>. Accessed on September 10, 2015.</sub>

b. "♦ my best friend as a writer. It tests you, to see if you have what it takes to see it through."
(Markus Zusak, Australian author)

<sub>Extracted from <www.brainyquote.com/quotes/quotes/m/markuszusa530347.html>. Accessed on September 10, 2015.</sub>

c. "♦ always ♦ to the core of my spiritual journey." (Henri Nouwen, Dutch clergyman)

<sub>Extracted from <www.brainyquote.com/quotes/quotes/h/henrinouwe588340.html>. Accessed on September 10, 2015.</sub>

d. "I have three friendships that have lasted a long time, but ♦ and gone." (Alexa Vega, American actress)

<sub>Extracted from <www.brainyquote.com/quotes/quotes/a/alexavega629389.html>. Accessed on September 10, 2015.</sub>

**2.** Read and identify the occurrences of the present perfect in the extract below. Then choose the alternative that best explains what the use of this verb tense indicates.

> "We call that person who has lost his father, an orphan; and a widower that man who has lost his wife. But that man who has known the immense unhappiness of losing a friend, by what name do we call him? Here every language is silent and holds its peace in impotence."
>
> (Joseph Roux, French clergyman)

<sub>Extracted from <www.brainyquote.com/quotes/quotes/j/josephroux100988.html?src=t_friendship>. Accessed on September 10, 2015.</sub>

- It indicates that the actions are happening at this moment.
- It indicates that the actions happened at a definite time in the past.
- It indicates we don't know when those actions happened.
- It indicates we are not sure whether or not those actions will happen again.

# Unit 5

## Genitive Case

De forma geral, o *genitive case* é formado pelo acréscimo do apóstrofo + -s ('s) ao substantivo (pessoas ou animais) para expressar posse. Observe os exemplos abaixo:

*That girl's name is Lisa.*

*Are they Ms. Cooper's students too?*

*The women's bathroom is on the right.*

Após substantivos no plural terminados em –s, acrescentamos somente o apóstrofo ('). Observe.

*Those dogs' tails are really long!*

Quando há mais de um possuidor e queremos indicar posse comum, inserimos 's após o nome do último possuidor; mas quando queremos indicar posse individual, inserimos 's após cada um dos possuidores. Veja.

*Danny and Andrea's children are on vacation.*

*Susan's and Amanda's brothers graduated last year.*

## Possessive Adjectives

*Possessive adjectives* são utilizados para indicar posse e posicionam-se antes dos substantivos. Observe as frases nos quadros abaixo.

| |
|---|
| Jill is **my** new classmate. |
| When is **your** birthday? |
| Marcos plans to throw a huge party on **his** 16th birthday. |
| My sister is looking forward to taking **her** finals. |

| |
|---|
| **Its** fur is a mixture of black and brown. |
| **Our** summer vacation will be fantastic! |
| You should never give up on **your** dreams. |
| Are these **their** flash drives? |

**1.** Read the text and find the elements that refer to possession.

> **coloured** (UK)
> **colored** (US)

### Festival de Tango: a guide to Buenos Aires Tango Festival

[...]

Buenos Aires and tango are about as inseparable as, well, a pair of tango dancers. In celebration of its sultry and mysterious dance, the Argentine capital stages this annual festival, with events spread out across the city. Dancers and musicians perform at various intimate venues, and it offers a great way to see some of the best tanguistas from around the world do their thing. Once you've been inspired, there's plenty of opportunity to discover tango for yourself. There are free classes for beginners throughout the 10 days of the festival, with thousands of wannabe Gardels stumbling through their first tango steps. To take part, simply turn up – you'll find a schedule of classes on the festival website. There are also classes for more advanced tanguistas; for these you must register through the website. There's a database of dancers seeking partners on the website if you need someone to swing.

Essentials: If you really want to get into step, best bring a partner... it takes two to tango, remember.

Local Attractions: Tango's master figure was Carlos Gardel and you can pay homage at his sarcophagus in the Chacarita cemetery. Pay a visit to blue-collar La Boca, with its homes and buildings coloured like lollipops.

[...]

Extracted from <www.lonelyplanet.com/argentina/buenos-aires/travel-tips-and-articles/76336>. Accessed on September 10, 2015.

# Language Reference

**2.** Read a text fragment about some festivals and celebrations in Japan. Then choose the correct options to complete it.

[...]

### Obon

Obon commemorates the return of the *ancestor' / ancestors / ancestors'* spirits to earth to visit their relatives. The Buddhist event, typically celebrated in mid-July or mid-August, depending on whether the solar or lunar calendar is observed, begins with the hanging of lanterns to guide the spirits to the home. Participants perform dances, make food offerings and visit the graves of *his / our / their* relatives. The festival culminates when observers set lanterns afloat to guide their ancestors back to the spirit world.

[...]

### Doll Festival or Hina Matsuri

March 3 marks Hina Matsuri, called the "Doll Festival" or "*Girls' / Girl is / Girl's*' Festival" in English, when families wish their daughters a happy and successful life. An elaborate display of dolls representing the emperor, *his / my / their* wife and the imperial court are displayed in homes during the festival. The dolls are offered rice crackers and other food. Hina Matsuri originated in the Edo period when the dolls were perceived to be charms that warded off evil spirits. Some Japanese families set paper dolls afloat to carry off bad luck. The Hina Matsuri display is taken down immediately after the holiday because traditional Japanese believe that those who do not will have trouble marrying off *her / its / their* daughters.

Extracted from <traveltips.usatoday.com/festivals-celebrations-japan-100386.html>. Accessed on September 10, 2015.

# Unit 6

## Present Perfect II

O *Present Perfect* é frequentemente usado com algumas palavras como:

- **Already**: empregado quando queremos expressar que determinada ação aconteceu antes do previsto; é posicionado entre *have / has* e o verbo principal em frases afirmativas.

  I have **already** tried Japanese food.

- **Ever**: usado quando queremos perguntar se alguma coisa aconteceu em algum momento até agora; é posicionado entre *have / has* e o verbo principal em frases interrogativas.

  Have you **ever** traveled to Hawaii?

  *Ever* também é usado após superlativos em frases afirmativas.

  You are the best friend I have **ever** had!

- **For** e **since**: utilizados para expressar ações que começaram no passado e continuam até o presente. *For* é posicionado antes de um período de tempo, e *since* é posicionado antes do início desse período.

  She has studied mechanical engineering **for** 2 years.
  She has studied mechanical engineering **since** she got married.

De maneira geral, usamos *for* e *since* em resposta a perguntas feitas com *How long*. Observe:

A: **How long** have they been married?
B: They have been married **since** 2013.

A: **How long** have you lived in this neighborhood?
B: We've lived here **for** 10 years.

- **Just**: usado quando nos referimos a uma ação que acabou de acontecer; posicionado entre *have / has* e o verbo principal.
  *Louis and Helen have **just** arrived from their trip to Cairo and they're throwing a dinner party tonight. Would you like to come?*
- **Lately / recently**: empregados para falar sobre ações ocorridas ultimamente ou recentemente.
  *Fernando has worked a lot **lately**.*
- **Never**: utilizado quando nos referimos a ações que não aconteceram em tempo algum antes; é posicionado entre *have / has* e o verbo principal em frases afirmativas, mas com sentido negativo.
  *Gosh! I'm sure it has **never** rained like this before.*
- **Yet**: usado quando queremos dizer que uma ação ainda não aconteceu até o momento em que se fala, mas espera-se que aconteça; é posicionado ao final de frases negativas ou interrogativas.
  *I haven't made lunch **yet**. I'm starting right now!*
  *Have you met the man of your dreams **yet**?*

**1.** Read the cartoons and check the statements that best explain them.

a.
- There has been a change in people's arguments since 1960.
- People have used the same arguments for years.
- People have discussed inter-racial marriage lately.

b.
- The mothers haven't decided yet whether to tell the man about how their baby was conceived.
- The mothers have just answered the man's question.
- The mothers and the man have never believed in science.

**2.** Complete the quotes below with the adverbs from the box.

| always | for | never | since |
|---|---|---|---|

**a.** "I'm a supporter of gay rights. And not a closet supporter either. From the time I was a kid, I have ♦ been able to understand attacks upon the gay community. There are so many qualities that make up a human being... by the time I get through with all the things that I really admire about people, what they do with their private parts is probably so low on the list that it is irrelevant." (Paul Newman, American actor).

Extracted from <www.goodreads.com/quotes/223672-i-m-a-supporter-of-gay-rights-and-not-a-closet>. Accessed on September 10, 2015.

**b.** "I think the record industry, by and large what's left of it, is still totally homophobic. I think it's ♦ less so in the film industry now, but the record industry, it's ♦ been a man's world." (Lesley Gore, American musician)

Extracted from <www.brainyquote.com/quotes/quotes/l/lesleygore305748.html>. Accessed on September 10, 2015.

Language Reference 177

# Language Reference

**c.** I, Binyavanga Wainaina, quite honestly swear I have known I am a homosexual ♦ I was five. (Binyavanga Wainaina, Kenyan author)

Extracted from <www.brainyquote.com/quotes/quotes/b/binyavanga625564.html>. Accessed on September 10, 2015.

**d.** "The issue of equal rights for lesbian, gay, bisexual and transgender individuals has vexed politicians ♦ decades. I have my own cloudy history with the issue, having supported a law in Mississippi that made it illegal for LGBT couples to adopt children. I believed at the time this was a principled position based on my faith." (Ronnie Musgrove, American politician)

Extracted from <www.brainyquote.com/quotes/quotes/r/ronniemusg525453.html>. Accessed on September 10, 2015.

## Comparatives

Flexionamos os adjetivos no grau superlativo, como estudamos no volume 1, e também no grau comparativo, ou seja, para comparar duas coisas, pessoas, lugares ou ações.

Para formarmos o comparativo de adjetivos de uma sílaba e de alguns adjetivos de duas sílabas, acrescentamos a terminação *-er* ao final.

> great – great**er**   nice – nic**er**
> ugly – ugl**ier**   fat – fat**ter**

Estude as regras ortográficas para formar adjetivos no grau comparativo:

- Adjetivos terminados em *-e* são acrescidos de *-r*: *nice – nicer*
- Adjetivos terminados em consoante + vogal + consoante têm a última consoante dobrada antes do acréscimo de *-er*: *fat – fatter*
- Adjetivos terminados em *-y* precedido por uma consoante perdem o *-y* e são acrescidos de *-ier*: *ugly – uglier*

Para formarmos o comparativo da maioria dos adjetivos de duas sílabas e de adjetivos com três ou mais sílabas, usamos a palavra **more** antes deles.

> important – **more** important
> intelligent – **more** intelligent
> handsome – **more** handsome

Observe os exemplos a seguir.

*Does she act as if she were **younger**?*

*I like cold days because they're **more romantic**.*

Note que há algumas formas irregulares de comparativos:

> good – **better**
> bad – **worse**
> far – **farther / further**

Usamos *than* quando mencionamos o segundo item da comparação.

*Sally is **prettier than** her sisters Laura and Michele.*

*Living in a big city isn't **more interesting than** living in a small town.*

1. Skim the text and identify one sentence that indicates comparison. Then read the whole text carefully and choose the appropriate answer.

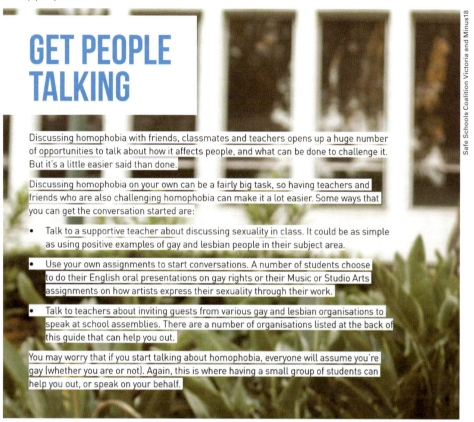

Extracted from <www.glhv.org.au/files/Stand%20Out.pdf>. Accessed on April 1, 2016.

a. This text is part of a guide that may have been distributed to Australian teachers with the aim of encouraging them to discuss homophobia with their students.

b. This text is part of a guide that may have been distributed to Australian students with the aim of encouraging them to discuss homophobia at school.

# Units 7 and 8

## Passive Voice

A voz passiva é normalmente usada quando a ação é mais importante do que o agente, quando falamos de uma verdade universal ou quando não é importante mencionar ou não sabemos dizer o que ou quem realizou a ação.

A voz passiva é mais comum na língua escrita e frequentemente empregada em textos jornalísticos ou documentos científicos.

Formamos a voz passiva usando o verbo *to be* no mesmo tempo verbal da voz ativa, mas acrescido do particípio passado do verbo principal. O sujeito da voz ativa torna-se o objeto da voz passiva e vice-versa.

Para mencionarmos quem ou o que realizou a ação, usamos a preposição *by*. Veja.

*Active Voice:* Jack prepares the food.

*Passive Voice:* The food is prepared by Jack.

Language Reference 179

# Language Reference

| Active Voice | Passive Voice |
|---|---|
| I **take** my puppy for a walk. | My puppy **is taken** for a walk (by me). |
| My dad **paints** houses. | Houses **are painted** (by my dad). |
| You **taught** Portuguese. | Portuguese **was taught** (by you). |
| Pamela **helped** homeless children. | Homeless children **were helped** (by Pamela). |
| We **must protect** the ones we love. | The ones we love **must be protected** (by us). |
| **Should** we **buy** a smartphone? | **Should** a smartphone **be bought** (by us)? |
| You **cannot** read that book. | That book **cannot be read** (by you). |
| **May** I **tell** the good news? | **May** the good news **be told** (by me)? |
| They **might not send** e-mails at school. | E-mails **might not be sent** at school (by them). |

**1.** Read the introduction of the "THINK! Road Safety Survey 2013" and find 5 passive voice occurrences. Then pick out the correct statements about the text.

> The THINK! Road Safety publicity campaign was launched in 2000, as part of the Government's road safety strategy, Tomorrow's roads: safer for everyone. A mix of engineering, enforcement and education measures were used, with THINK! Road Safety communications activity supporting the achievement of a 44% reduction in the number of people killed or seriously injured between 2000 and 2009 when compared to the 1994-1998 baseline.
>
> The Government published a new strategy document, Strategic Framework for Road Safety in May 2011. This strategy aims to continue making progress in reducing road deaths and serious injuries through safer infrastructure, education drawing on behavioural science and tougher, targeted sanctions at both the national and local level, with a greater emphasis on more local, devolved decision making. THINK! continues to be part of this strategy.
>
> The THINK! campaign aims to encourage all road users to recognise that it is the small things they do that can lead to crashes on the road and that there are simple steps they can take to reduce their risk to themselves and others. THINK!'s power is that it fosters an attitude of shared responsibility. THINK! campaign priorities are identified by the Department for Transport's publicity team in collaboration with policy officials in the Road User Safety Division. They are chosen because they account for the highest number of road casualties and it is felt that they will benefit most from coordinated national publicity.

Extracted from <webarchive.nationalarchives.gov.uk/20140322101948/https://www.gov.uk/government/uploads/system/uploads/attachment_data/file/251297/think-annual-survey-2013.pdf>. Accessed on September 10, 2015.

**behavioural** (UK) / **behavioral** (US)
**recognise** (UK) / **recognize** (US)

  a. A new strategy document Strategic Framework for Road Safety was published by the Government in May 2011.
  b. 44% more people were killed or seriously injured between 2000 and 2009 if we compare to the 1994-1998 baseline1.
  c. An attitude of shared responsibility is fostered by THINK!

**2.** Read the poster and complete its corresponding passive voice statement.

Innocent people ♦ by drunk driving.

Extracted from <quotesgram.com/dui-posters-quotes/>. Accessed on September 10, 2015.

**3.** Choose the correct alternative to complete the text below.

> Child trafficking is child abuse. Children ♦, moved or transported and then exploited, forced to work or sold.
>
> Children ♦ for:
> - child sexual exploitation
> - benefit fraud
> - forced marriage
> - domestic servitude such as cleaning, childcare, cooking
> - forced labour in factories or agriculture
> - criminal activity such as pickpocketing, begging, transporting drugs, working on cannabis farms, selling pirated DVDs, bag theft.
>
> Many children are trafficked into the UK from abroad, but children ♦ from one part of the UK to another.

Extracted from <www.nspcc.org.uk/preventing-abuse/child-abuse-and-neglect/child-trafficking/what-is-child-trafficking/>. Accessed on September 10, 2015.

a. are recruited / trafficked / is also trafficked

b. was recruited / are trafficked / are also trafficked

c. are recruited / are trafficked / can also be trafficked

d. should be recruited / is trafficked / can also be trafficked

**4.** Match the columns to complete the quotes.

a. "Children must be

b. "The soul is

c. "Every child comes with the message that God is not yet

- taught how to think, not what to think." (Margaret Mead, American anthropologist)
- discouraged of man." (Rabindranath Tagore, Bengali poet)
- healed by being with children." (Fyodor Dostoyevsky, Russian novelist)

Extracted from <www.compassion.com/poverty/famous-quotes-about-children.htm>. Accessed on September 10, 2015.

# Audio Scripts

## Track 2, page 21, activities 2 and 3

This is the colonial city of Bahia, known as the black capital of Brazil. The place where millions of African slaves were first brought to South America. Brazilians love to show off their Afro-Brazilian culture with the Capoeira and the famous Baianas. A country that's long boasted of being a nation living in mixed race harmony.

But, while Brazil may look color-blind, people know that's an illusion.

I sell health insurance policies for a company that's on the ninth floor of that building, but when I went to take a white client upstairs, the building administrator said, "no, you have to take the stairs. You cannot ride the elevator."

Many would have done nothing, but Silva reported the incident to the Justice Ministry's Office against Discrimination.

Here, we have always denied the existence of racial discrimination. We confuse racial coexistence with racial equality.

Blacks and browns, or *pardos* as they are called here, make up nearly half the population of this country. In fact, Brazil has the largest black population in the Western Hemisphere, but you would never know it by looking at who holds positions of power. "That", says this Bahia state congressman, "is what proves that Brazil is not a racial democracy."

We make up 84% of the population of Bahia, but never in our history have we had one black governor. Where blacks are over represented is in the slums like Morro do Borel in Rio de Janeiro, where we met Monica Santos, a community leader who's studying social sciences at university.

Monica is one of the beneficiaries of a controversial new quota system to guarantee university access to blacks who currently make up only 2.2% of the student population.

I thought it would be rose-colored, but the resistance and racism of many professors here is fierce. They say that if you come from the ghettos, you are not fit to study certain subjects like philosophy, for example, because people like us have an intellectual deficit.

One hundred and twenty years after Brazil abolished slavery, one thing is changing. The awareness that this is, after all, a color-coded country. (0:00 - 2:40)

Lucia Newman, Al Jazeera, Bahia, Brazil

Transcribed from <www.youtube.com/watch?v=AASusCA0XVA>.
Accessed on August 8, 2015.

## Track 3, page 35, activity 2

Today, on this 100th anniversary of International Women's Day, we celebrate a century of progress, a century of women using their collective voice to organize for change.

It is very appropriate that at the same time, we are celebrating the creation of UN Women, an ambitious international commitment to accelerate the realization of women's rights and gender equality.

I am honoured to be the first leader of this new United Nations organization.

Much has been achieved over 100 years. When the first International Women's Day took place, women could vote only in two countries. Today, that right is virtually universal and women have now been elected to lead Governments in every continent. Women are participating in the workforce in greater and greater numbers and 67 countries have laws mandating equal pay for men and women; 126 countries have guaranteed maternity leave.

As we see on our television screens every day, women and girls are mobilizing, alongside men and boys, to advance political freedoms worldwide. While the achievement of gender equality is closer than ever before, we still have far to go.

Our vision in UN Women is a world where men and women have equal opportunities and capacities and the principles of gender equality are embedded in the development, peace and security agendas.

Realizing this vision involves opening up spaces for women's political leadership, as trade and peace negotiators, as heads of corporations; it involves freeing women from gender-based violence and convincing key policy makers that where women fully contribute to their economies and societies, the gains for everyone are greatly increased.

Evidence shows that where women have access to good education, good jobs, land and other assets, national growth and stability are enhanced, and we see lower maternal mortality, improved child nutrition, greater food security and less risk of HIV and AIDS. Men and women around the world who share this vision have a new global champion in UN Women to help make our collective vision a reality.

I am determined that UN Women will live up to the hopes of those who worked so hard to establish it, and will generate new energy, bringing together people from every country, society and community in a shared endeavour.

Happy International Women's Day! (0:00 - 3:07)

<small>Extracted from <www.unbrussels.org/component/content/article/41-reports/253-international-womens-day-video-message-by-un-women-executive-director-michelle-bachelet.html>. Accessed on October 25, 2015.</small>

## Track 5, pages 54 and 55, activities 2 and 3

Chants from indigenous people getting ready for competition; indigenous tribes from all over Brazil pouring into the city of Cuiabá to take part in the twelfth edition of the Indigenous Games.

They'll compete in traditional sports, bow and arrow, blow dart competition and wrestling, among others. Football breaks with the tradition, but it is an event. This is Brazil after all.

In previous years, in canoeing we were champions, and in the tug of war we got to the finals, but lost. But this year we came to try to win the games.

We came here to share with other tribes that are our brothers too. We are going to integrate among different ethnicities and meet new tribes.

The World Cup and Olympics are coming to this country, but there's a case to be made – it's the Indigenous Games that are the most colorful. What they lack in big sponsorship or multi-million-dollar TV deals, they make up for with passion. This is the biggest cultural gathering of indigenous people in Brazil, and it's held every other year. There are more than fifteen hundred indigenous people from more than forty tribes taking part in these games, but for them it's about a lot more than simply competition.

It's our tradition. It's our culture. This is why we came from so far away, to share our culture with the outside world.

But before the games can begin, they participate in a ceremonial fire dance to celebrate being together.

Filling the air, tribal song and dance; energy that will be transformed into bouts of athleticism in the coming days. (0:00 - 1:54)

Gabriel Elizondo, Al Jazeera. Cuiabá, Brazil

<small>Transcribed from <www.youtube.com/watch?v=O2D_-JXJ9qs>. Accessed on August 20, 2015.</small>

## Track 7, page 68, activity 2

Hello again, and welcome to another happiness podcast with me, Frederika Roberts, the happiness speaker. Today, I want to talk to you about friendship, and the importance of friendship.

As I'm recording this podcast, I'm ridiculously excited, elated, exhilarated even, because this evening, I am driving a couple of hours to go and see a very good friend of mine, Claire, who lives very close to Manchester airport, which is very handy on this occasion, because I'm going to spend a few of hours with her this evening, crash at her house, and sneak out before dawn to catch an early morning flight to Rome.

Now you would think going to Rome would be exciting enough, and of course it is, even though I've been [there] many, many times; I'm so fortunate I have a lot of family there. To me, going to Rome on this occasion is about so much more than the beautiful, the magical, the stunning city of Rome, with which I am absolutely head over heels in love. For me, going to Rome this time marks a special occasion. [...] (0:00 - 1:11)

<small>Transcribed from <audioboom.com/boos/1647579-friendship-is-fundamental-to-happiness>. Accessed on August 20, 2015.</small>

## Track 8, page 69, activity 3

[...] Now, I grew up in Luxembourg with friends from all over Europe originally, and my two closest and oldest, and I'm not saying oldest in terms of age – we're still very young at 40 and 41 between us –, but my oldest friends stemming back to when we were four and in kindergarten, in nursery, have gone through the entire school life with me. And, we were so close, and we've continued to be close even though we've lived in different countries for the past 23 years, since we all finished school. And, it's not very often that we spend a lot of time with each other. Errr, usually, when I go to Luxembourg over Christmas, which is every couple of

# Audio Scripts

years, we manage to… to snatch a few of hours with each other. Claire lives in Brussels now. Yes, it is another Claire. I have a lot of Claires in my life. And Nadège lives just over the border from Luxembourg in Germany now, but to all intents and purposes, it's as if she lives in Luxembourg in terms of visiting.

And, here's the thing, it's never enough time. When we see each other, it's as if we'd never left off. We just pick up and carry on all the usual conversations, and that's a true mark of friendship. We're there for each other no matter what. We always have been, over the years, regardless of the distance. But, the last time we had any serious time together was when Nadège was pregnant with Mika, her second child, and that was quite a few years ago now. So, the opportunity came up. My cousin's flat is empty for a little while, before she moves into it, and since the person that was renting it has moved out, and although I do have family and my mum has a flat in Rome, we wanted a space that was ours. So, we decided to just get together and have long weekend in Rome, as we all had to fly, so it didn't really matter where we were gonna go, as long as it was reasonably short haul, and not too expensive. So, that's why I'm so excited, because I'm so blessed. I'm so fortunate I have these amazing friends in my life. (1:12-3:18)

Transcribed from <audioboom.com/boos/1647579-friendship-is-fundamental-to-happiness>. Accessed on August 20, 2015.

### Track 9, page 89, activities 3 and 4

Augusto and I are back in Floresta for the climax of *Bumba-meu-boi*. So, this is the time when all the various groups come together, and they show the rest of the city what they've been preparing.

Yeah, today's a big night for the many groups here, because, errr, we celebrate St. Peter's Day. Yeah, it's the most important day here for the Maranhão people, yeah.

Clutching their emu feathers and their costumes, the people of Floresta take the bus to the city.

There's an air of nervousness as the time approaches for their moment in the public spotlight.

They needn't have worried. Their performance is fantastic. As I watch Nadir and the troupe take the stage, I'm really moved by the spirit and the quality of their performance. They tell the story as it should be told. With their richly embroidered costumes, and original and inventive masks, there's a real feeling of a community creating something out of nothing.

The Florestans may come from one of the poorest parts of the city, but tonight they take over the old streets of São Luís. They shine the brightest. (0:00 - 1:57)

Transcribed from <https://www.youtube.com/watch?v=gHuOcKOHoFE>. Accessed on August 22, 2105.

### Track 10, page 102, activity 2

My birth mother, she was 18 when, uhm, she was pregnant with me, and she couldn't... uhm, or with her family situation, she wasn't able to take care of a child that she thought, so she wrote a letter, uhm, to this agency, saying that she wanted to put her child up for adoption when... uhm... when she gave birth. And so my parents at the time, they were looking for someone to work with them, like a lawyer to work with them, or an adoption agency. But uhm, everyone rejected them because they were gay. My birth mother, she was looking through the binder that had all the letters of parents who would like to adopt or people who would like to adopt and become parents, and she loved their letter. So they met. She loved them. She said that... I want you to be the parents of my child (1:37 – 2:21)

[...]

We're just a great family. We all get along. You know... we always have fights, as all families have fights and our ups and downs. But, you know, we're all very open with each other. And I'm very, I feel very comfortable talking with my parents about anything. We... we do family, like singing time and I play the piano, so if I play and my pop plays the guitar and then my dad sings along. And we do that, and another thing that we do... that I know a lot of my friends actualy don't do is we sit down together. We eat dinner together and we talk. And... and, that's just a great way to, like, catch up on what we've done during the day. And so that, that's just a few things that we like to do as a family (2:59 – 3:37).

Transcribed from <www.youtube.com/watch?v=Z9xfHqT1HEY>. Accessed on April 18, 2016.

### Track 11, page 103, activity 4

I think, uhm... Because recently, you know, the whole idea of same-sex marriage in the United

States and everywhere. I think it's affected me because my friends are talking about it too. And then it's... it's interesting hearing their opinions on it. And then, like, students and classmates... it's, it's really interesting hearing what they have to say. 'Cause some people, I thought, you know, they were cool with my family. But then when it comes to same-sex marriage, they have a different opinion. They're like, well, I don't, you know, I don't think they should get married. You know, I think things are fine the way they are. But they don't realize that, you know, they're talking about my family, too (3:50 – 4:26)

[...]

I think one thing that I would say to people, who maybe don't have LGBT parents or, you know, are just in schols though, that uhm, where kids around them are LGBT or have LGBT parents... you know, just be aware of your surroundings. Be aware of things you say. And, because, it might hurt the people around you. And you know, we're no different. We're all the same, you know, in the sense that we all just wanna be kinda cared for. We all wanna be loved. And uhm, just kind of be aware of your surroundings and try to make them more comforta... a more comfortable place and a safer place for everyone (4:30–5:03)

Transcribed from <www.youtube.com/watch?v=Z9xfHqT1HEY>. Accessed on April 18, 2016.

## Track 13, page 122, activity 2

Did you know that 41% of kids have had at least one alcoholic drink by the age of 14 or that 2.6 million teens don't know that you can die from an alcoholic overdose?

My name is Kaitlyn Stoneburner, and I'm here to give you the facts on underage drinking.

The average age when kids first try alcohol is eleven years old for boys and thirteen years old for girls.

45% of people who begin drinking alcohol before the age of 14 become dependent on alcohol at some point in their lives. Many teens do binge drinking, meaning they have five or more drinks at a time. Binge drinking can destroy your liver, cause heart disease, and even cause a coma or death. Alcohol can damage every organ in your body. It is absorbed directly into your blood stream and can increase your risk for many life-threatening diseases, including Alzheimer's and cancer.

Natasha Farnham was born and raised in England, but she started drinking when she was only twelve years old. By the time she was 13, she was drinking up to six bottles of wine a day. A year later, Natasha was diagnosed with liver failure and almost died. Now 18, she still suffers from permanent memory loss and has to take daily medicines to help repair her liver.

You don't have to be the one drinking to get hurt, though. If you are around people that have been drinking, you have a greater risk of being involved in car crashes and affected by alcohol-related violence. An estimated 7000 people under the age of 21 die each year from alcohol-related injuries. In 2002, 29% of people aged 15 to 20 who had died in car crashes had been drinking.

Drinking will slow your reflexes, affect your coordination, and cause distorted vision, memory lapses, and even blackouts.

When polled on their reasons for drinking, 66% of teens said that they drink because of peer pressure. What they don't know is that alcohol is actually a depressant, not a stimulant, and it's the main factor in 75% of all day rapes.

There are ways to tell if you have a serious problem. Do you drink more than you mean to? Have your problems with school, work or relationships gotten worse since you started drinking? If you have a friend or loved one who needs help, tell an adult or an authority figure immediately. The highest rates of underage drinking are in rural and suburban areas, not just big cities. If you or someone you know has a problem with alcohol abuse, visit www.niaaa.nih.gov or call 1-800-662-HELP. That's 1-800-662-4357. There's always someone that wants to help. (0:00 - 3:15)

Transcribed from <www.youtube.com/watch?v=Gb1duJVHETQ>. Accessed on September 3, 2015.

## Track 14, page 122, activity 3

Did you know that 41% of kids have had at least one alcoholic drink by the age of 14 or that 2.6 million teens don't know that you can die from an alcoholic overdose?

# Audio Scripts

My name is Kaitlyn Stoneburner, and I'm here to give you the facts on underage drinking.

The average age when kids first try alcohol is eleven years old for boys and thirteen years old for girls.

45% of people who begin drinking alcohol before the age of 14 become dependent on alcohol at some point in their lives. Many teens do binge drinking, meaning they have five or more drinks at a time. Binge drinking can destroy your liver, cause heart disease, and even cause a coma or death. Alcohol can damage every organ in your body. It is absorbed directly into your blood stream and can increase your risk for many life-threatening diseases, including Alzheimer's and cancer. (0:00-1:04)

Transcribed from <www.youtube.com/watch?v=Gb1duJVHETQ>.
Accessed on September 3, 2015.

## Track 15, page 122, activity 4

Natasha Farnham was born and raised in England, but she started drinking when she was only twelve years old. By the time she was 13, she was drinking up to six bottles of wine a day. A year later, Natasha was diagnosed with liver failure and almost died. Now 18, she still suffers from permanent memory loss and has to take daily medicines to help repair her liver.

You don't have to be the one drinking to get hurt, though. If you are around people that have been drinking, you have a greater risk of being involved in car crashes and affected by alcohol-related violence. An estimated 7000 people under the age of 21 die each year from alcohol-related injuries. In 2002, 29% of people aged 15 to 20 who had died in car crashes had been drinking.

Drinking will slow your reflexes, affect your coordination, and cause distorted vision, memory lapses, and even blackouts.

When polled on their reasons for drinking, 66% of teens said that they drink because of peer pressure. What they don't know is that alcohol is actually a depressant, not a stimulant, and it's the main factor in 75% of all day rapes.

There are ways to tell if you have a serious problem. Do you drink more than you mean to? Have your problems with school, work or relationships gotten worse since you started drinking? If you have a friend or loved one who needs help, tell an adult or an authority figure immediately. The highest rates of underage drinking are in rural and suburban areas, not just big cities. If you or someone you know has a problem with alcohol abuse, visit www.niaaa.nih.gov or call 1-800-662-HELP. That's 1-800-662-4357. There's always someone that wants to help. (1:05-3:21)

Transcribed from <www.youtube.com/watch?v=Gb1duJVHETQ>.
Accessed on September 3, 2015.

## Track 17, page 137, activities 2 and 3

In the early 1900s, children were used as laborers for two main reasons: There were no strongly enforced laws against child labor, and they could be paid even less than adults. In 1910, it was easy to find school-aged kids like Furman Owens, who started working in a South Carolina mill when he was only eight. He said he and others like him didn't even know their ABCs, and that they wanted to learn, but they couldn't because they worked all the time.

Individual workers and social reformers in the 1800s and 1900s fought against child labor, dangerous working conditions, long hours, and bad wages. But they had little power until labor unions were formed.

Striking was an effective bargaining tool. But going on strike was not just a parade. It was more like a rebellion, and the situation could be terrifying and dangerous. Local and national governments treated strikes as civil unrest and often dispatched armed troops to break them up. Workers were injured, and many died as they clashed police and National Guard.

Unions worked very hard to demand legislation that brought about an end to child labor in this country. Unions over the years have fought for legislation to protect workers on the job but also to protect the living conditions, the living standards of working people.

Transcribed from <https://www.youtube.com/watch?v=s9U4Vx6ImpE>.
Accessed on April 20, 2016.

# Extra Resources

## Unit 1

Read about the absence of black and mixed people in stadiums during the 2014 World Cup in Brazil at

<www.theguardian.com/commentisfree/2014/jul/01/brazil-black-faces-crowd-rainbow-nation-world-cup>. Accessed on August 8, 2015.

Watch a video clip performed by a hip-hop artist, which has been launched by the Australian Human Rights Commission to send an anti-racism message to young people. Duration: 4:25

<www.racismnoway.com.au/archive/initiatives/brotherblack-antiracism-video.html>. Accessed on August 7, 2015.

*Pride and Prejudice*. [Orgulho & Preconceito]. 2005. Duration: 129 minutes

Directed by Joe Wright and based on a novel by Jane Austen, the movie tells the story of Elizabeth Bennet, who meets and falls in love with Dr. Darcy, a rich and proud man.

## Unit 2

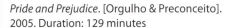

Read an article about the main female leaders in Latin America at

<www.diplomaticourier.com/latin-america-s-leading-ladies/>. Accessed on August 10, 2015.

This article gives you a global perspective on women in corporate boardrooms. The article refers to many countries, including Brazil.

<www2.deloitte.com/content/dam/Deloitte/global/Documents/Risk/gx-ccg-women-in-the-boardroom.pdf>. Accessed on August 10, 2015.

Watch a video about one of the keys to alleviate poverty: women's and girl's empowerment. Duration: 2:03

<www.youtube.com/watch?t=68&v=qrO2yskc62w>. Accessed on August 10, 2015.

Listen to *Women of the World*, a song written by Nick Weaver for the International Women's Day 2015

Available at <www.youtube.com/watch?v=iVKRKUYdcNE>. Accessed on August 10, 2015.

## Unit 3

Read about Brazilian Indians and learn about living tribes, their history, and where they live

<www.survivalinternational.org/tribes/brazilian>. Accessed on August 10, 2015.

Read about Mário Juruna's death in *The New York Times*

<www.nytimes.com/2002/07/19/world/mario-juruna-58-only-indian-to-serve-in-congress-in-brazil.html>. Accessed on August 10, 2015.

Watch the video *Stranger in the Forest*, which is about tribes recalling their experiences of contact with civilization and the dangers they faced. Duration: 8:48 minutes

<www.survivalinternational.org/tribes/uncontacted-brazil>. Accessed on August 7, 2015.

## Unit 4

Read an article about how to make friends, keep them and how friends make our lives better

<www.helpguide.org/articles/relationships/how-to-make-friends.htm>. Accessed on August 17, 2015.

AUSTEN, Jane. *Pride and Prejudice*. New York: Penguin Books, 2009.

Read about the strong friendship ties between Elizabeth Bennett and Charlotte Lucas, as well as about the tight love bond between Elizabeth and Mr. Darcy.

ALCOTT, Luisa May. *Little Women*. New York: Leatherbound Classics, 2012.

Read about the true friendship among the sisters Meg, Jo, Beth and Amy in this novel. Their unconditional love and unbreakable bond is inspiring.

# Extra Resources

## Unit 5

Read about the history and folklore of São Luís, MA.
<gobrazil.about.com/od/braziliancities/ss/Sao-Luis.htm>. Accessed on August 23, 2015.

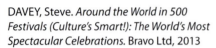
DAVEY, Steve. *Around the World in 500 Festivals (Culture's Smart!): The World's Most Spectacular Celebrations.* Bravo Ltd, 2013
The book explores the richness of 500 festivals that take place around the world every year and helps people who are willing to attend a festival.

## Unit 6

Watch a video with Zach Wahls, a 19-year-old University of Iowa student, speaking about his two mothers and the strength of his family in the Iowa House of Representatives. Duration: 3 minutes
<www.youtube.com/watch?v=FSQQK2Vuf9Q>. Accessed on August 25, 2015.

Read the book summary of *My Two Moms* by Zach Wahls and Bruce Littlefield at
<www.openlettersmonthly.com/book-review-my-two-moms/>. Accessed on August 25, 2015.

Read about gay marriage around the world at
<www.pewforum.org/2015/06/26/gay-marriage-around-the-world-2013/>. Accessed on November 23, 2015.

## Unit 7

Get further information about the minimum legal drinking age around the world
<drinkingage.procon.org/view.resource.php?resourceID=004294>. Accessed on September 4, 2015.

Get to know about the *What You Can't See* campaign, which aims at clearly explaining the damages alcohol can cause to the human body
<alcoholthinkagain.com.au/Campaigns/Campaign/ArtMID/475/ArticleID/12/What-You-Cant-See>. Accessed on September 5, 2015.

Watch a 4-minute animation about how alcohol damages the teenage brain.
<www.turningpoint.org.au/Education/Schools-and-Young-People/Under-Construction.aspx>. Accessed on September 4, 2015.

## Unit 8

For further information about children's rights in Brazil, access
<www.loc.gov/law/help/child-rights/brazil.php>. Accessed on September 7, 2015.

Take a look at this website and get to know what child labour free zones are and where to find them
<www.stopchildlabour.eu/child-labour-free-zones/>. Accessed on September 7, 2015.

# Irregular Verbs List

| Base Form | Past | Past Participle | Translation |
|---|---|---|---|
| be | was, were | been | ser, estar |
| become | became | become | tornar-se |
| begin | began | begun | começar |
| break | broke | broken | quebrar |
| bring | brought | brought | trazer |
| build | built | built | construir |
| catch | caught | caught | pegar |
| choose | chose | chosen | escolher |
| come | came | come | vir |
| cut | cut | cut | cortar |
| deal | dealt | dealt | lidar |
| do | did | done | fazer |
| draw | drew | drawn | atrair (audiência) |
| drink | drank | drunk | beber |
| drive | drove | driven | dirigir |
| eat | ate | eaten | comer |
| feel | felt | felt | sentir |
| fight | fought | fought | lutar |
| find | found | found | achar |
| fly | flew | flown | voar |
| forget | forgot | forgot(ten) | esquecer |
| forgive | forgave | forgiven | perdoar |
| get | got | got(ten) | conseguir |
| give | gave | given | dar |
| go | went | gone | ir |
| grow | grew | grown | crescer, cultivar |
| have | had | had | ter |
| hear | heard | heard | ouvir |
| hold | held | held | realizar; segurar |
| hurt | hurt | hurt | machucar |
| keep | kept | kept | guardar |
| know | knew | known | conhecer; saber |

| Base Form | Past | Past Participle | Translation |
|---|---|---|---|
| lead | led | led | conduzir; gerenciar |
| leave | left | left | deixar, partir |
| let | let | let | permitir |
| lose | lost | lost | perder |
| make | made | made | fazer |
| mean | meant | meant | significar |
| meet | met | met | encontrar |
| overcome | overcame | overcome | superar |
| pay | paid | paid | pagar |
| put | put | put | pôr |
| read | read | read | ler |
| ride | rode | ridden | andar (de elevador) |
| rise | rose | risen | subir, erguer-se |
| run | ran | run | correr |
| say | said | said | dizer |
| see | saw | seen | ver |
| seek | sought | sought | procurar |
| sell | sold | sold | vender |
| send | sent | sent | enviar |
| set | set | set | ajustar, marcar |
| sit | sat | sat | sentar |
| speak | spoke | spoken | falar |
| spend | spent | spent | gastar; passar |
| swim | swam | swum | nadar |
| take | took | taken | levar |
| tell | told | told | dizer |
| think | thought | thought | pensar |
| throw | threw | thrown | arremesar; atirar |
| understand | understood | understood | entender |
| wake up | woke up | waken up | acordar |
| wear | wore | worn | vestir, usar |
| win | won | won | vencer, ganhar |
| write | wrote | written | escrever |

# Glossary

**accept:** aceitar
**acceptance:** aceitação
**accurate:** correto(a), preciso(a)
**acknowledgment:** confissão
**advice:** conselho
**advice column:** coluna de aconselhamento
**advice letter:** carta solicitando aconselhamento
**advise:** aconselhar, recomendar
**advocate:** defensor(a)
**agree:** concordar
**agreement:** acordo
**aim:** visar; objetivo
**ambition:** ambição
**animosity:** animosidade
**ashamed:** envergonhado(a)
**attend:** frequentar
**awareness:** conscientização
**ball:** baile
**be out on your own:** viver de forma independente/por conta própria
**be safe:** estar protegido(a), salvo(a), seguro(a)
**bear:** trazer
**behavior:** comportamento
**benefit:** benefício; beneficiar, favorecer
**besides:** além de
**beyond:** além de
**binge drinking:** consumo excessivo de álcool
**biography:** biografia
**bladder:** bexiga
**body brace:** colete ortopédico
**bog:** pântano
**bone marrow:** medula óssea
**bow and arrow:** arco e flecha
**bowel:** intestino
**brain:** cérebro
**bribery:** suborno

**brought up:** criado(a); educado(a)
**bull:** touro
**businessperson:** empresário(a)
**canoeing:** canoagem
**cardboard box:** caixa de papelão
**caring:** cuidado, preocupação, zelo
**catchy:** atraente; cativante
**change:** alteração, mudança
**chorus:** refrão
**claim for:** reivindicar
**coming out:** o ato de reconhecer a própria homossexualidade
**commission:** encomendar
**commit:** cometer
**commitment:** compromisso
**communal:** comunitário(a)
**companionship:** companheirismo
**comparison:** comparação
**conceive:** conceber
**consent:** consentimento, permissão
**consumption:** consumo
**contrast:** contraste
**convey:** transmitir
**counselor:** conselheiro(a)
**crown jewel:** o mais importante
**custom:** costume, hábito, tradição
**cycle back down:** cair em depressão
**dart:** dardo
**date:** data; namorar
**decision-making:** tomada de decisões
**dedication:** dedicação
**deprived:** carente; desprovido(a); necessitado(a)
**deputy:** deputado(a)
**develop:** desenvolver
**development:** desenvolvimento
**disappoint:** decepcionar
**discrimination:** discriminação
**disguise:** disfarçar

**donor:** doador(a)
**doubt:** dúvida
**down-to-earth:** prático(a), realista
**draft:** rascunho
**drinker:** aquele que bebe
**due to:** devido a
**earthy:** mundano
**embroidered:** bordado(a), enfeitado(a)
**endeavor** (US) / **endeavour** (UK): empenho, empreendimento, esforço
**engaged:** comprometido(a)
**ensure:** garantir
**every now and then:** de vez em quando
**exemplification:** demonstração; exemplificação
**exploitation:** exploração
**exquisite:** extraordinário(a)
**face:** enfrentar; rosto
**fancy ball:** baile a fantasia
**feel like:** ter vontade de; sentir-se
**feeling:** sentimento
**fictional name:** nome fictício
**finding:** descoberta
**first:** em primeiro lugar, primeiramente
**foetal development:** desenvolvimento fetal
**for instance:** por exemplo
**fortunate:** afortunado(a)
**foster home:** casa de acolhimento, lar adotivo
**friendship:** amizade
**galvanize:** alarmar
**garb:** traje
**gather:** coletar, acumular
**gender:** gênero
**genuine:** sincero(a)
**get along:** dar-se bem (com alguém)
**governance:** gestão

# Glossary

**growth:** crescimento
**guide:** guiar
**guilty:** culpado(a)
**hall:** corredor, saguão
**harm:** prejudicar; dano, mal, prejuízo
**holy:** sagrado(a)
**however:** contudo
**in power:** no poder
**increase:** aumentar; aumento
**inference:** inferência, conclusão
**injury:** dano, ferimento, lesão
**inspiration:** inspiração
**integrity:** integridade
**issue:** assunto; problema; questão
**join:** unir
**jungle:** floresta
**key:** fundamental; principal; solução
**knowledge:** conhecimento
**labor** (US) / **labour** (UK): trabalho
**land:** terra
**landmark:** marco, ponto de referência
**laugh:** rir
**law:** lei
**leader:** líder
**leadership:** liderança
**legend:** lenda
**lent:** quaresma
**line:** verso (de música)
**liver:** fígado
**loaded:** cheio(a) de
**long-drawn-out:** prolongado(a)
**look up to:** admirar
**lower house:** câmara dos deputados
**lyrics:** letra de música
**mandate:** mandato
**maternity leave:** licença-maternidade
**measure:** medida
**metaphor:** metáfora

**miscarriage:** aborto
**neglect:** rejeitar; rejeição
**news report:** reportagem
**on-the-job:** no trabalho
**out-of-date:** obsoleto, fora de moda
**outside:** fora (de), do lado de fora
**overall:** de modo geral
**overview:** panorama, visão geral
**overwhelming:** esmagador(a)
**part-time job:** emprego de meio expediente
**pattern:** exemplo, modelo, tipo
**peoples:** povos
**plaintiff:** demandante
**portray:** retratar
**pregnancy:** gravidez
**pregnant:** grávida
**prejudice:** preconceito
**previously:** previamente
**private:** particular
**provide:** oferecer
**punishment:** pena, penalidade
**purpose:** propósito, objetivo, finalidade
**quote:** citação
**racist:** racista
**raised:** criado(a), educado(a)
**record:** gravar; registrar
**refer:** referir
**refuse:** recusar
**reiterate:** reiterar
**relationship:** relacionamento
**renowned:** renomado(a)
**reply letter:** resposta (carta)
**request:** pedido
**research:** pesquisa
**respect:** respeito
**revelry:** festança, folia
**right:** direito; correto(a)
**role model:** exemplo, modelo

**sacred:** sagrado(a)
**second:** em segundo lugar
**secular:** mundano(a), profano(a)
**set up:** instalar, iniciar (negócio)
**slave:** escravo(a)
**slavery:** escravidão
**solidarity:** solidariedade
**source:** fonte
**span:** estender sobre
**spastic cerebral palsy:** paralisia cerebral espástica
**spread:** difundir, propagar; difundido(a), propagado(a)
**stereotype:** estereótipo
**stillbirth:** natimorto
**straight friend:** amigo heterossexual
**strength:** força
**struggle:** esforço, luta
**stunning:** deslumbrante
**survive:** sobreviver
**throng:** multidão
**throughout:** em toda parte, do começo ao fim
**trafficking:** tráfico
**travel guide:** guia de viagem
**treasure:** tesouro
**tribe:** tribo
**underage:** menor de idade
**understanding:** compreensão
**up-to-date:** atualizado
**updated:** atualizado(a)
**upscale:** sofisticado(a)
**vagrancy:** vida errante
**value:** valor
**venue:** espaço, local (de um evento ou atividade)
**will:** desejo, vontade
**without:** sem
**workforce:** mão de obra
**workplace:** local de trabalho

# Bibliography

ABREU-TARDELLI, L. S.; CRISTOVÃO, V. L. L. (Org.). *Linguagem e educação*: o ensino e aprendizagem de gêneros textuais. Campinas: Mercado de Letras, 2009.

BEZERRA, M. A.; DIONISIO, A. P.; MACHADO, A. R. (Org.). *Gêneros textuais & ensino*. São Paulo: Parábola Editorial, 2010.

BRASIL/SEMTEC. *PCN+ Ensino Médio: Orientações educacionais complementares aos Parâmetros Curriculares Nacionais*. Volume 1: Linguagens, códigos e suas tecnologias. Brasília, DF: MEC/SEMTEC, 2002. Disponível em: <portal.mec.gov.br/seb/arquivos/pdf/02Linguagens.pdf>. Acesso em: 12 julho 2015.

BRASIL/SEMTEC. *Linguagens, Códigos e suas Tecnologias: Orientações Curriculares para o Ensino Médio. Capítulo 3. Conhecimentos de línguas estrangeiras*. 2006. Disponível em <portal.mec.gov.br/seb/arquivos/pdf/book_volume_01_internet.pdf>. Acesso em 12 julho 2015.

COPE, B. & KALANTZIS, M. Multiliteracies: The Beginning of an Idea. In: COPE, B. & KALANTZIS, M. (Eds.). *Multiliteracies: Literacy Learning and The Design of Social Futures*. London: Routledge, 2000. p. 3-8.

CROSS, D. *Large Classes in Action.* Hertfordshire: Prentice Hall International, 1995.

DIONISIO, A. P. et al. (org.) *Gêneros textuais & ensino*. Rio de Janeiro: Lucerna, 2002, p. 19-36.

Diretrizes Curriculares Nacionais da Educação Básica. Ministério da Educação, 2013.

FREIRE, Paulo. *Pedagogia da autonomia*: saberes necessários à prática educativa. São Paulo: Paz e Terra, 1996.

GRELLET, F. *Developing Reading Skills.* Cambridge: Cambridge University Press, 1981.

HEIDE, Ann & STILBORNE, Linda. *Guia do professor para a internet*: completo e fácil. Trad. Edson Furmankiewz. 2. ed. Porto Alegre: Artmed, 2000.

HOFFMANN, Jussara. *Avaliar para promover: as setas do caminho*. Porto Alegre: Mediação, 2001.

LAPKOSKI, G. A. O. *Do texto ao sentido*: teoria e prática de leitura em língua inglesa. Curitiba: Ibpex, 2011.

MARCUSCHI, L. A. "Gêneros textuais: definição e funcionalidade". In: DIONISIO, A. P. et al. (org.) *Gêneros textuais & ensino*. Rio de Janeiro: Lucerna, 2002, p. 19-36.

MARTINEZ, P. *Didática de línguas estrangeiras*. São Paulo: Parábola Editorial, 2009.

MOITA-LOPES, L. P. "Ensino de inglês como espaço de embates culturais e de políticas da diferença." In: GIMENEZ, T. et al. (Org.). *Perspectivas educacionais e o ensino de inglês na escola pública*. Pelotas: Educat, 2005.

_____. *Oficina de linguística aplicada*. Campinas: Mercado de Letras, 2000.

RAIMES, A. *Techniques in Teaching Writing*. New York: Oxford University Press, 1983.

RICHARDS, J. C.; RENANDYA, W. A. (Ed.). *Methodology in Language Teaching*: an anthology of current practice. New York: Cambridge University Press, 2002.

RODRIGUES, D. (Org.). *Inclusão e educação*: doze olhares sobre a educação inclusiva. São Paulo: Summus, 2006.

ROJO, Roxane; MOURA, Eduardo. *Multiletramentos na escola*. São Paulo: Parábola Editorial, 2012.

SCHNEUWLY, Bernard & DOLZ, Joaquim. *Gêneros orais e escritos na escola*. Campinas: Mercado das Letras, 2004.

SOUZA, Adriana Grade Fiori et al. *Leitura em língua inglesa*: uma abordagem instrumental. São Paulo: Disal, 2005.

TOMLINSON, B. *Developing Materials for Language Teaching*. Londres: Continuum, 2003.

VYGOTSKY, L. S. *Pensamento e linguagem*. São Paulo: Martins Fontes, 1993.

WALESKO, A. M. H. *Compreensão oral em língua inglesa*. Curitiba: Ibpex, 2010.